The Struggle for Inner Peace

Henry Brandt

A revised, updated edition of *The Struggle for Peace*

While this book is designed for the reader's personal enjoyment and profit, it is also intended for group study. A leader's guide with Victor Multiuse Transparency Masters is available from your local bookstore or from the publisher.

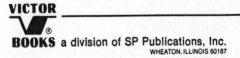

VICTOR

BOOKS a division of SP Publications, Inc.
WHEATON, ILLINOIS 60187

Offices also in
Whitby, Ontario, Canada
Amersham-on-the-Hill, Bucks, England

Recommended Dewey Decimal Classification: 248.4
Suggested Subject Heading: CHRISTIAN LIFE: BEHAVIOR.

Library of Congress Catalog Card Number: 83-51312
ISBN: 0-88207-245-5

Originally published as *The Struggle for Peace,* © 1965
    by SP Publications, Inc.
Revised edition, © 1984 by SP Publications, Inc. All rights reserved
Printed in the United States of America

VICTOR BOOKS
A division of SP Publications, Inc.
            Wheaton, Illinois 60187

Contents

Preface

This book, first published in 1965, stated my views on mental health, on knowing yourself, on inner peace. The book was based on 12 years' experience in private counseling practice and in it, I attempted to integrate my secular education, biblical studies, and experience in trying to help real people with real problems. Many people struggle to find inner peace, and my effort has been to help them find it through Jesus Christ, the source of peace. He said, "Peace I leave with you, My peace I give to you; not as the world gives do I give to you. Let not your heart be troubled, neither let it be afraid" (John 14:27).

I believed that Christ was the source of peace when I wrote this book, and now, 19 years later, I am more convinced than ever. This "revision" needed very little revising. Much of what I wrote originally, I wrote by faith. Now, from my own experience, from observing the lives of hundreds of fellow earthly travelers, and from interacting with thousands of clients, I can add fact to faith and reaffirm the truths contained in these pages. I see more clearly now than I did then that we are the architects of our own troubles and fears. I've also discovered we are more prone to seek peace in the world than I realized 19 years ago.

In revising this book I considered updating quotations, but decided that more recent quotations did not add to the originals. However, some facts and figures have been updated.

I am indebted to Homer Dowdy, who helped crystallize the ideas and outline for the original book and who assisted me editorially. Homer was busy with the Food for the Hungry organization and writing a biography, so he could not help with this revision. Ms. Elizabeth Oldenborg, who assisted with research, has gone to be with the Lord. Eva, my wife of 42 years, who helped with the first typing, has also gone on to heaven. Now I am indebted to Marcella, my wife of three months, for her help with the editing and typing. Authors and publishers are recognized appropriately throughout the book.

This book is addressed mainly to Christians—those who have acknowledged that they are sinners: "Whoever commits sin also commits lawlessness, and sin is lawlessness" (1 John 3:4). "All have sinned and fall short of the glory of God" (Rom. 3:23).

Christians recognize that they cannot save themselves: "The wages of sin is death, but the gift of God is eternal life in Christ Jesus our Lord" (Rom. 6:23). "For by grace you have been saved through faith, and that not of yourselves; it is a gift of God, not of works, lest anyone should boast" (Eph. 2:8-9).

Christians, in true repentance, have asked Christ to be their Saviour: "This is a faithful saying and worthy of all acceptance, that Christ Jesus came into the world to save sinners, of whom I am chief" (1 Tim. 1:15). "Repent therefore and be converted, that your sins may be blotted out, so that times of refreshing may come from the presence of the Lord" (Acts 3:19). "There is no other name under heaven given among men by which we must be saved" (Acts 4:12).

But the Bible indicates that Christians, even though they

have believed in and received Christ for salvation, still sin. "My little children, these things I write to you, that you may not sin. And if anyone sins, we have an Advocate with the Father, Jesus Christ the righteous. And He Himself is the propitiation for our sins, and not for ours only but also for the whole world" (1 John 2:1-2).

Many Christians hold hatred, fear, resentment, jealousy, and malice toward others. As a result, fellowship with these persons and the Lord is broken, joy is lost, and God's peace is not enjoyed. Confessing and forsaking one's sinful ways in obedience to the Lord and His Word are necessary if the Christian is to enjoy God's peace: "He who covers his sins will not prosper, but whoever confesses and forsakes them will have mercy" (Prov. 28:13). "If we confess our sins, He is faithful and just to forgive us our sins and to cleanse us from all unrighteousness" (1 John 1:9).

This book is written with the hope that many Christians will be helped in their "struggle" for inner peace, released from anxiety, and experience the "fruit of the Spirit" which includes peace (Gal. 5:22).

I pray sincerely that God may use this book to help you in your daily struggle and that you will find abiding peace through Jesus Christ. "The God of peace be with you" (Rom. 15:33).

1
Mental Health—
Whose Problem?

Rachel Baker was a bundle of nerves. She could not sit still for long. She would pace the floor, and toss and turn in bed at night, unable to sleep. Her family and friends wondered what was wrong with her. She would, for no apparent reason, suddenly break off a conversation, turn away as if angry, and refuse to say anything more to them.

She had gone to her physician because she was nervous. After a thorough examination he assured her that her nervous system was all right, and that there was nothing wrong with her body's organs. He said some problem must be troubling her.

At the advice of her physician she came to our clinic for counseling. Knowing her history of "nervousness" from the referral, I proceeded to discover the reason.

"Are you having any difficulties?"

Mrs. Baker was quite surprised. "That's what my doctor asked me."

Are you?"

"No, I don't have any problems."

"How are you getting along with your husband?"

"Oh, fine," she replied.

"Any problem with the children?"

"No."

"Or with your parents?"

"No."

"In-laws?"

"No."

"Neighbors?"

"No."

We were having a fast-moving conversation. She was answering my questions promptly—too promptly—without even giving them a passing thought. It is not unusual for a reluctant client to respond this way.

"Are you here because you wanted to come?" I asked.

"Frankly, no," she said, "I'm here because my physician insisted. To level with you, I'm disgusted to be here. What can talking to you possibly do for my nerves? Does my physician think I'm a mental case?"

She answered my last question with lots of feeling and more than her usual terse reply. There was a lively person under that indifferent front after all.

"You must have an ideal life," I ventured.

"Well, no," she replied, smiling faintly. "I wouldn't exactly say that."

"Then what about it is not ideal?"

She thought for a few seconds, then volunteered: "Well, I'd be a little happier if my husband were more considerate."

I encouraged her to be specific.

"To be truthful, there are a number of things he does that put a damper on the happiness of our home," she said. She went on to explain that her marriage had not turned out just the way she thought it would. In fact, she said, there were many ways her husband failed to measure up.

"If his friends only knew the way he treats me!"

By her tone and choice of words she was implying a selfish, heartless brute of a man.

"In what ways is he inconsiderate?" I asked. She did not reply, and was silent for nearly two minutes. Finally she said: "I can't seem to think of anything definite right now."

I asked her to think awhile longer. It wasn't necessary to talk just to fill a gap in our conversation. So she sat quietly for several minutes. Eventually she spoke.

"I'm a little embarrassed—oh, it's not anything I should bring up. I mean it's kind of small, but anyway, you asked me to be specific, so I'll tell you what comes to my mind.

"It started early in our marriage. You see, we have a tooth-brush holder in the bathroom. I'm left-handed so I've always liked to hang my toothbrush in the slot farthest to the left. He's right-handed, and he knows I'm used to that slot. But time after time, where do I find his toothbrush? In my slot!"

She apologized again for bringing up such a trivial thing, but said it did remind her of something else.

"It's the washbowl. Do you think he'll wipe it out when he's through shaving? Indeed not! And the towels—when I ask him to put clean ones out, he hangs them on the racks with a horizontal fold instead of a vertical." And that, she indicated, was enough to upset anybody.

There was more. Her father had always gone down to the kitchen before the rest of the family and had the toast ready when they came to breakfast. But not her husband. He never got near the toaster.

"I try and try to get him to match his tie with his suit, but he goes to work looking like a rainbow if I don't catch him before he leaves the house."

At the start she had presented her husband as an awful individual. But like many people who describe their antago-nists in broad, accusing terms, she could come up with no more serious indictment than faulty toothbrush storage when asked to be specific.

Often a person seeking counsel will describe a mate as someone against whom the counselor should be protected by a bodyguard. But when the mate turns up for an interview, he proves to be quite a gentleman (or lady)—and with some complaints of his (or her) own. This was the case with Mrs. Baker's husband, Floyd.

"She complains when I raise the bedroom window a half inch," he said one day when it was his turn to speak. He liked to watch the ball game on television, but she always chose that time to talk to him.

"I'm not against a man talking to his wife," he said, "but why on earth can't she wait till the game is over?"

Her answer: "If he loved me, he'd put me ahead of his old ball game." She believed that if he'd just cut out his irritating ways there would be no problem between them. I asked him why he didn't.

"Because she won't change the ways she annoys me," he said.

They were caught in a vicious circle, a pattern that had developed in their marriage because of the habits each had brought into it.

Who would link a dislocated toothbrush to nervousness? Yet, add the dirty washbasin, and the towels, and the toast, and the mismatched necktie, and the windows, and the television sports, and you have battlegrounds in the bathroom, kitchen, bedroom, and living room, as well as at the front door. On top of these, minor eruptions pile up centering on the church, the neighbor's children, and the checkout clerk at the supermarket.

Some irritants are more annoying than others. Take the skirmish over the ball game on television. He knows she'll try to distract him the minute he turns on the game, so he is tempted to delay going home and to ask himself where else he can watch television. She thinks to herself, *Oh brother! It's almost time for him to come home and turn on that horrid game.*

Even before Floyd and Rachel see each other at the end of the day, they are already sparring for mastery (and no one has yet fought a battle without raising a host of emotions). They brought this pattern of behavior into their marriage. The slightest issue became a debate. To lose a decision was considered a bitter defeat. To win a decision was sweet victory. But in victory there is always a loser, and losing is an irritant.

The tiniest loss, even if it is a minor issue, can be extremely irritating. A speck in your eye is not a serious problem, but it is so annoying that it takes all your attention until it is removed. A grain of sand is nothing, but put enough grains together and you have a ton of sand. So it is with one's response to conflict. Each irritant becomes far heavier than its own weight. As one piles on another, they blend into a vague blob, and all the irritable person is aware of is "nervousness."

Mrs. Baker consulted her doctor because she was a bundle of nerves. He sent her to me because he learned that her "nerves" were caused by an emotional rather than a physical problem. In other words, she was not adjusting well to people or events in her life. This is commonly called the "mental health" problem.

The Key to Emotional Wellness

George Preston, in his little book, *The Substance of Mental Health,* (Rinehart, p. 112) says the essential quality for mental health is to live (1) within the limits of one's bodily equipment, (2) with other human beings, (3) happily, (4) productively, and (5) without being a nuisance.

A widely circulated pamphlet published by the National Association for Mental Health (New York, N.Y. 10019) is titled,

"Mental Health Is . . . 1 2 3." People with good mental health, the pamphlet says, feel comfortable about themselves, feel right around other people, and are able to meet the demands of life. It adds that mentally healthy people are good friends, good workers, good mates, good parents, and good citizens.

The Bible gives us a comparable picture of a Christian who draws his strength from God:

> The fruit of the Spirit is love, joy, peace, long-suffering, kindness, goodness, faithfulness, gentleness, self-control (Gal. 5:22-23).
>
> Since you have purified your souls in obeying the truth through the Spirit in sincere love of the brethren, love one another fervently with a pure heart (1 Peter 1:22).
>
> Distributing to the needs of the saints, given to hospitality (Rom. 12:13).
>
> Fulfill my joy by being like-minded, having the same love, being of one accord, of one mind (Phil. 2:2).

The Uneasy Generation

Interacting with friends, workers, mates, and children will reveal the inner workings of a person. Being irritable can cause bodily aches and pains, tiredness, nervousness. The mind can become weighed down by burdens. Granted, the irritants may be small, vague ones. All a person may say is, "I'm anxious, afraid." Maybe he can't tell you any particular thing that is bothering him. But he knows something is, and once in a while one particular sore will fester till it breaks open.

This vague uneasiness typifies our society today. Here and there are noticeable spots showing that all is not well in our makeup. The crime rate is growing; juvenile delinquency is increasing; racial violence and dangerous international tension are heightening. Half of our hospital beds are said to be occupied by persons having mental or emotional difficulties. But these are only the bulges of a weak inner tube. More trouble spots will likely be revealed in days to come.

Record rates are being run up in divorce, drug addiction, and alcoholism. I wrote this paragraph in 1965. What has happened since then? Look at some statistics which are undoubtedly even more startling today than when they were compiled. According to the National Center for Health, in 1979 there were 1.18 million divorces granted—three times more than the 395,000 granted in 1959. The center estimates that 1.18 million children under 18 had parents who were involved in a divorce in 1979 compared to 562,000 children in 1963.

On March 3, 1983 I was startled by reading in the Cleveland *Plain Dealer* that 45 percent of the 1981 births in that city were to unwed mothers. In 1980, births out of wedlock in Baltimore totaled 57 percent; Chicago, 45 percent; and Detroit, 43 percent.

The First Statistical Compendium on Alcohol and Health, published in February 1981 by the U.S. Department of Health and Human Services, gives us some chilling data on alcohol consumption. In 1975, there were about 7.5 million alcoholics in the United States. In 1970, our Veterans Administration hospitals discharged 53,396 or 7.7 percent of all patients whose principal diagnosis was alcoholism. By 1977, the number of alcoholics had climbed to 101,342 or 10.8 percent of all discharges. In 1977, approximately 50 percent of all murders, sexual assaults, and robberies were alcohol-related. In 1975, 50,000 people died in car accidents; 35 to 64 percent of the drivers in those fatal accidents had been drinking. There were 1.5 million people injured in alcohol-related accidents.

In 1978, 2.60 gallons of spirits, 2.51 gallons of wine, and 29.78 gallons of beer were consumed for each person above legal drinking age (18 and older). Eleven percent or 17.8 million people 18 or older are heavy drinkers—meaning two or more drinks a day.

The economic costs of our alcohol consumption are fright
ening:

Loss of production	$19.64 billion
Health and medical	12.74 billion
Car accidents	5.14 billion
Violent crime	2.86 billion
Fire loss	.43 billion
Social responses	1.94 billion
Total	$42.75 billion

There is also the growing dependence on addicting drugs.
Senator Dan Quayle (R-Indiana) reported these findings of the
Labor and Human Resources Committee. From 3 to 7 percent
of the employed population use some form of illicit drug,
ranging from marijuana to heroin, on a daily basis. Marijuana
appears to be the principal substance of use and accounts
for 90 percent of current users. Amphetamines are used 34
percent of the time; barbituates, 21 percent; and heroin, 5
percent.

Employees with a drinking or drug problem are absent 16
times more than the average employee, have an accident rate
four times greater, use a third more sickness benefits, and have
five times more compensation claims while on the job (*American Psychologist*, April 1983, p. 455).

It's Happening to Christians!

Millions of people are suffering from chronic worry, hypertension, prejudice, guilt, hatred, fear, and the harassment of failure.
In their struggle for inner peace, a quick solution is to turn to
alcohol and drugs.

An alarming number of people suffering from these ailments
are professing Christians! The person who knows Christ as

Saviour is not immune to mental or emotional problems. He is as susceptible to tension and anxiety as a non-Christian work- ing beside him at the office or plant or living next door.

If you are struggling with a difficulty, you are not alone. That is, you are not the only one facing a problem, even though you share your inner conflict with no one.

"My problem is so simple," you say. "How can I talk about it? I can see that I'm mad at my wife. But when I think of the inconsequential things over which I'm mad, I get confused. Why should I lose my temper over a misplaced pair of socks, or why would I leave the house upset because she disapproves of my bowling teammates?

"But the way I am—my reactions to life at home, at work, at church, with my relatives—cause me to lose sleep at night, to lash out at the children, to say things I don't mean. I think thoughts that surprise me. I tell myself, 'This can't be me.' "

You can see the vague outline of your problem, but you cannot figure it out. You look at a skyscraper and may get the impression that some magician has had a hand in putting together this magnificent, massive structure. But if you had seen it being erected, you would know it was built of relatively small pieces of material—a length of steel, a pane of glass, a copper pipe, a bolt, a weld, a switch, the particles that make up concrete. The problems you face are constructed quite similarly.

While living in the shadow of your problems, you look on them as massive, unexplainable. As you dismantle them to see what they're made of, you're a little embarrassed to find their components are so simple and ordinary. So you do nothing. Nothing, that is, till the problems overwhelm you. Then those who know you say, "He blew up," or "She's upset," or "He's suffering from a breakdown."

Emotional Ills and Physical Ills

How widespread is emotional disturbance? We have cited the statistic that about half of the patients in our hospitals have become ill due to mental or emotional problems. For every person committed to a mental institution, a dozen are outside, groping in a half-real world. Ours is the age of anxiety, the age of the tranquilizer. We celebrate National Mental Health Week.

W.C. Alvarez, of the Mayo Clinic, says:

> Even after 53 years of practicing medicine, I still keep marveling at the fact that so many people whose discomforts are nervous in origin have failed to see any connection between their physical ills and the severe emotional crises that they have been going through.
>
> A thousand times when I have drawn from some nervously ill patient his story of sorrow, strain, great worry, or paralyzing indecision, he has looked at me puzzled and asked "Could it be *that?*" Like so many people he has never realized that many illnesses— even severe ones—are produced by painful emotion (*Live at Peace with Nerves,* Prentice-Hall, pp. 5-6).

Such people *are* sick. Ulcers are eating their stomachs; chronic headaches are driving them to distraction; chest pains have them frightened nearly to death. So not only are they mentally confused, but physically sick. And because they are sick, their conditions are assumed to be in the realm of the medical physician. After all, when people can't sleep because of the pains in their necks or their stomachs won't hold food, the help of medicine certainly seems called for.

Through the years, the close association between our emotions and physical symptoms has made it easy to assume that the symptoms were caused by some disease or by a body organ that has not been working correctly. Lately, however, it is becoming increasingly clear that the roots of such symptoms lie in the individual's adjustment to people. One spokesman for this view is T. S. Szasz, a leading New York psychiatrist, who says:

> Psychotherapy is being widely practiced as though it entailed nothing other than restoring the patient from a state of mental sickness to one of mental health. While it is generally accepted that mental illness has something to do with man's social (or interpersonal) relations, it is paradoxically maintained that problems of values (that is, of ethics) do not arise in this process. Yet, in one sense, much of psychotherapy may revolve around nothing other than the elucidation and weighing of goals and values— many of which may be mutually contradictory—and the means whereby they might best be harmonized, realized, or relinquished ("The Myth of Mental Illness," *The American Psychologist,* February 1960, p. 113).

Another articulate spokesman, O. H. Mowrer, psychologist at the University of Illinois, said some years ago,

> The only way to resolve the paradox of self-hatred and self-punishment is to help the individual see he deserves something better. As long as he remains hard of heart and unrepentant, his conscience will hold him in the viselike grip of neurotic rigidity and suffering. But if at length the individual confesses his past stupidities and errors and makes what poor attempts he can at restitution, then the conscience will forgive and relax its stern hold and the individual will

be free, "well." But here too we encounter difficulty, because human beings do not change radically until they first acknowledge their sins, but it is hard for one to make such an acknowledgment unless he has "already changed." In other words, the full realization of deep worthlessness is a severe ego "insult," and one must have a new source of strength to endure it ("Sin, the Lesser of Two Evils," *The American Psychologist,* May 1960, p. 301).

Mowrer thus calls attention to one of the great barriers to finding relief from anxiety and guilt—a sense of deep worthlessness that is indeed a severe ego insult. We tend to shrink away from the truth about ourselves.

Drs. Szasz and Mowrer clearly describe our tendency to wander away from sensible and righteous behavior. We all act stupidly and make errors. The Bible reminds us that "all have sinned" (Rom 3:23) and "there is none righteous" (Rom. 3:10). The Bible says our sins are against God. As the psalmist put it: "Against You, You only, have I sinned, and done this evil in Your sight—that You may be found just when You speak, and blameless when You judge" (Ps. 51:4).

Dr. Szasz sees our salvation in harmonizing, realizing, or relinquishing goals and values. Dr. Mowrer sees our salvation in squaring our past stupidities and errors with our own consciences by making attempts at restitution. Unfortunately, human relief is not the same as God's forgiveness, cleansing, and renewal.

God's Answer
The struggle for peace is just that—recognizing and dealing with the sin that causes your problem. Paul Tournier, a Christian psychiatrist in Switzerland, says everyone experiences guilt feelings and seeks to escape them by self-justification and

repression of conscience. "To tear men from this impossible situation and to make them capable once more of receiving grace, God must therefore first of all awaken within them the repressed guilt" (*Guilt and Grace,* Harper and Row, p. 142).

Sometimes, Tournier explains, this arousal comes only through severe dealings which are necessary to lead men to the experience of repentance and grace. He writes, "For a man crushed by the consciousness of his guilt, the Bible offers the certainty of pardon and grace. But to one who denies this it bears terrible threats in order to make him introspect himself" (*Guilt and Grace,* p. 145).

Tournier then refers to God's words in the Book of Jeremiah: "I will bring judgment upon you because of your saying, 'I have not sinned' " (Jer. 2:35, MLB). The aim of "operation severity," Tournier says, "is not the crushing of the sinner but, on the contrary, his salvation. For that, God must pull him out of the vicious circle of his natural attempts at self-justification" (*Guilt and Grace,* p. 146).

In coming to terms with yourself, you must consider your relationships to the people and events in your life. Because mental health is related to your attitudes toward people, it is not a matter primarily for the physician. The Bible—not medical books—holds the key. God's Word deals with one's relationships with others, with standards of conduct, with emotions, with the deep issues of life, with the heart of a man before God.

The struggle for peace is a spiritual matter, involving your soul or spirit and how you react to the things that come your way. The source of peace involves your relationship to God.

2
Discovering Yourself

Discovery, a fascinating, satisfying experience—but sometimes oh, so painful! So Jack and Ann found it.

They met during a college football game, then started dating. In walking Ann to class and in taking her to parties and games, Jack discovered some things about this girl. He quickly learned that she was a very neat person. Her clothes fit perfectly and were never wrinkled. Her papers were always carefully written. He heard from the girls in the dorm that her room was always straightened, her closet in order.

One day Jack found out that Ann was like this despite a careless roommate. Ruth was inclined to let her bed go unmade and her clothes lie in a heap. But she did not remain untidy for long. Ann kept after Ruth about her responsibilities. Sometimes Ruth complained to Jack that Ann was too fussy. But Jack had to admire Ann's stand. After all, how can you argue with someone who takes the lead in keeping things neat, even to the point of doing the job herself when her roommate fails?

Jack also had great respect for Ann's academic achievements, and even greater respect for the *way* she got her good grades. Ann was a serious student. Nothing came ahead of the books. He often wished he had just half her drive.

He was too easily satisfied with just getting by. But things began to change after they became better acquainted. He felt she inspired him.

"Let's unwind over a pizza," he would say after classes.

"Let's work on your English Literature first," she'd reply.

Jack never paid too much attention to his appearance till Ann opened his eyes to the pulled threads of his sweater or his need for a haircut. He began consulting her on how to dress properly for a particular kind of date. Also, Ann got him back into church. He had become lax, but now always went with her—and they arrived on time.

What more could anyone ask? When a fellow improves his appearance, raises his grades, becomes more punctual, and gets interested in church, isn't it all to the good? Jack was quite intrigued that a girl had done so much for him, and only slightly annoyed that without her he had been unable to see himself as he really was.

Their courtship was casual, quite uneventful. They talked everything over and settled all issues. Once in awhile, however, Jack had to admit to himself that he found relief in getting back to his room where he could relax, sprawl if he wanted, pick things up only when he felt like it—but, even so, her way was better.

Shortly after graduation they were married. The ceremony went off flawlessly. Ann's mother had thought of every detail; the music, the procession, the vows, the reception—all ticked off with clocklike precision.

Having majored in business administration, Jack was soon hired by a large company as a management trainee. Ann got a job teaching fourth grade. Together their paychecks were ample to allow them a nice apartment and many extras.

One night at Jack's suggestion, they went out to look at

cars. He wanted to see the new models; she thought they ought to limit themselves to a used car. He had long dreamed of someday owning a beautiful, powerful new car, and only reluctantly did he put aside the idea. Ann reminded him that they needed to save their money to buy a house, and he could see that she was right.

Jack had a way of coming home from work, settling down on the sofa, and kicking off his shoes. Quietly, Ann would pick up the shoes and put them in the closet. After a short nap Jack would jump up and feel for his shoes.

"Where are my shoes?" he would call, loudly enough for Ann to hear him in the next room.

Ann never shouted. She would come to the living room and say very evenly, "In the closet, Dear."

Jack habitually peeled off his suit coat and draped it over a chair. When he wanted it again—no coat.

"Where's my coat?" he would bellow impatiently.

And again Ann would come to the room and answer, "In the closet."

She was quiet, steady, dependable. How could you quarrel with her way of life? Because she was the way she was, Jack always bit off the harsh words on the tip of his tongue. It was better that way.

Dinner was always on the table at 6 o'clock sharp. At times Jack would sleep till 6, then wash up. Invariably, Ann would be seated. He would mumble an apology for being late, and grace would sound a little forced.

By the second year of their marriage they had saved enough to make the down payment on a house. How hard it had been to get together on a location, then on a specific model. They came closer to an argument over those decisions than over anything in the past. Once the house was built, they lacked furnishings. Jack wanted to buy what they needed on credit; Ann convinced him that this wasn't wise. So they moved in the few pieces of furniture they owned. The living room looked empty to Jack, and he wondered how long it would take to make this house look like a home.

He decided to have the yard sodded, but Ann called his notion extravagant. "You can seed it yourself after work," she said.

About this time a coolness began to develop between them. The usual hug-and-kiss greeting no longer provided the plea- sure it once had. They kept up the ritual, but it became a chore. Because conversation at times threatened to border on contro- versy, long silences developed.

They were glad to spend their evenings reading, watching television, attending church functions, visiting friends—any- thing to keep from talking to each other. Each was afraid to ask the other, "What's wrong?"

Neither could put a finger on any real issue between them. Yet something seemed to separate them. They ought to talk more, they decided, since each knew that communication was important to a successful marriage. So they talked more, though often silence was preferred. In one of their long talks they settled once and for all that there was no unresolved issue between them. They kissed, declared their love for each other, and agreed sincerely that they saw eye to eye. Yet each knew something was wrong.

Jack and Ann felt frustrated. They were an educated, dedi- cated, ambitious couple who shared common goals, were ac- tive together in church, and were loyal to each other. What was this quiet, mysterious, sinister force that threatened their marriage?

When they came for counseling, Ann said, "Dr. Brandt, we prefer to be together as we talk to you."

"That's right," joined her husband. "You see, we do every- thing together. We have nothing to hide from each other."

That first session was a puzzling one. I could come up with

no clue to their trouble. There were no issues, no unresolved problems. Only one suggestion occurred to me.

"Will you watch for any differences of opinion that may arise this week and pay attention to your reactions?" I asked. "And will you try to review your life together to see if there can possibly be any unresolved problems?"

Ann broke in: "I'm sure there are none. We love each other and solve any problem as soon as it comes up."

"That's true," said Jack, right behind her. "Are you suggesting that we aren't honest and open with each other?" Turning to his wife he said tenderly, "You are open with me, aren't you, Ann?"

Her answer was to nestle in his outstretched arms. They looked at me as if I were an enemy seeking to drive them apart.

Surprisingly, they were back the next week. Neither had seen any sense in it. Yet that nagging coolness remained, and they had to admit that something was wrong, something they either could not or would not see. Gently but firmly I urged them to try again to discover it.

"If there is an ache in your body, something is wrong," I reminded them. "No matter how reluctant you are to admit it, you must find and correct the trouble to get rid of the ache. Coolness between people is like an ache. Something is wrong. This may be a frightening idea, and you may prefer that it did not exist; but you cannot wish trouble away. You must get at it by uncovering the cause and removing it."

Next week they returned. Ann asked to see me alone. She entered the consulting room, closed the door, slumped into a chair, buried her face in her hands, and began to cry uncontrollably.

What had happened?

She had made a discovery, and not a pleasant one.

The past week had been rainy. Their lawn still wasn't in, so naturally mud was tracked into the house. Tuesday was an especially trying day in the classroom, and she knew she had to go to a church meeting that night. She was tired—worn out physically, fed up with the mud that seemed to be everywhere. As she stood at the kitchen sink peeling potatoes for dinner, she heard a car pull up in the rutted driveway. That would be Jack. The door opened and slammed.

"Take off your shoes on the landing!" she shouted, too tired to go to the stairs as she usually did. She heard one shoe fall, then the other. Jack came into the kitchen; absentmindedly she asked, "Did you take your shoes off?"

Using ample lung power he shot back, "Yes I took my shoes off!"

Ann broke into tears. "You don't need to shout at me."

"You don't need to shout at me either," he snapped. He was furious.

Jack wavered between two impulses. One was to take her in his arms; the other was to run. He ran. Into the bathroom he went, slamming the door behind him. Once there, he felt ashamed and confused. Not knowing what to do, he slipped into the living room and hid behind the evening paper.

Ann called dinner at 6 as usual. Jack went silently to his chair. Grace was said under considerable strain. Jack looked up to see Ann's eyes were red and swollen. She looked so pathetic, but he was frozen in his chair. There was nothing he could think of to say. Ann had nothing to say. So they didn't talk about the incident. And they hadn't brought it up since, till Ann mentioned it in her interview with me alone.

Later Jack came into the office for a private talk. I told him that Ann had shared with me the shouting episode. He was upset.

"She told you about *that?*" He had assumed she would keep such things to herself. *He* certainly would have. Then he assured me that their spat was only an isolated incident. Why make a mountain out of a molehill?

That was a good question. So I turned it back to him. "Why make a mountain out of a molehill?"

"What do you mean?" he asked.

"For an isolated incident, aren't both of you carrying this rather far?"

Jack became thoughtful. Perhaps I was right, he said ruefully. This little incident had created a thick wall between them. A week of silence followed during which neither exerted an effort to make up. At the next visit Ann had little to say except to remark that Jack seemed very distant. The whole situation was muddled to her. She just couldn't think.

Jack was more talkative. He had done some thinking, and he didn't like what he was coming up with. During the week his mind had wandered back to their courtship days. Yes, he had admired Ann's neatness. He had also entertained a thought or two in those days that maybe she was a bit too fussy. But he had never allowed so unkind a thought to linger. Now, by contrast, he thought more frequently of her fussiness, and he found himself dwelling on the thought.

He remembered how Ann constantly prodded her college roommate to be neat. *Now,* he was thinking, *she's keeping after me in the same way.* He realized that he resented the push.

Oh sure, Ann had changed his whole life for the better. But when she hadn't pushed him into a change, she had pulled him.

I asked Jack if he had shared his thoughts with his wife.

"Are you kidding?" He was amazed at my question.

"Why don't you?"

"No," he smiled, but not happily. "I don't think that's a good idea." Jack apparently had forgotten telling me during our first session that they talked everything over and he had nothing to hide from Ann. No doubt they both believed what they were saying. It is indeed true that a person can deceive himself. According to the Bible: "The heart is deceitful above all things, and desperately wicked; who can know it? 'I, the Lord, search the heart, I test the mind, even to give every man according to his ways, and according to the fruit of his doings' " (Jer. 17:9-10).

Evidently, when Jack and Ann said they shared everything, they meant sharing what they thought would not disturb the other. To return to my interview with Jack, I asked "How would Ann take it if you shared your thoughts with her?" He didn't know and would not even consider talking to her as he had talked to me. In fact, he felt terribly guilty for having told me such things. His wife was a wonderful woman. He owed a lot to her; she had inspired him to work hard, to set wise goals for his life, to take his responsibility as a Christian seriously. If it hadn't been for her, he might have drifted far away from the Lord. But after he said all that, the resentments of her fastidiousness, her bossiness, her pushing were still there.

Toward the end of our session, I called attention to the Apostle Paul's goals as outlined in Philippians 3:12-15. Paul realized that he was not perfect. Still he was open to learning. This willingness to know and to be known was what he called perfection. He added that for anyone who would be perfect, God would reveal any reluctance to know or to be known. Look at his exact words:

> Not that I have already attained, or am already perfected; but I press on, that I may lay hold of that for which Christ Jesus has also laid hold of me.
>
> Brethren, I do not count myself to have apprehended; but one thing I do, forgetting those things which are behind and reaching forward to those things which are ahead, I press toward the goal for the prize of the upward call of God in Christ Jesus.
>
> Therefore let us, as many as are mature, have this mind; and if in anything you think otherwise, God will reveal even this to you (Phil. 3:12-15).

"Maturity," I told Jack, "is not having arrived, but the will to see new light. Personal growth and development is based squarely on an honest look at yourself with the intent to correct any failings you may discover."

Getting to Know Me

The starting point is self-discovery. The psalmist wanted to know himself, and he knew it would take God to help him do it: "Search me, O God, and know my heart; try me, and know my anxieties; and see if there is any wicked way in me" (Ps. 139:23-24a).

How do you discover yourself?

Through their marriage Ann and Jack learned some things about themselves. Parents get to know their true selves through experiences with their children. Some persons get glimpses of themselves through working for or alongside others. The intense competition of sports will mirror the character of an athlete. Your relationships with people and your responses to the events of life will bring into focus both your qualities and your blemishes, both your strong points and your weaknesses.

You can see yourself in the Bible, "a discerner of the thoughts and intents of the heart" (Heb. 4:12). The Bible is profitable for doctrine, reproof, correction, and instruction in righteousness (2 Tim. 3:16). It provides you with a knowledge of sin (Rom. 3:20) and an understanding and a hatred of false ways (Ps. 119:104).

Through the eyes of your friends you can find out much about yourself. Jesus said to rebuke one who wrongs you, being ready, of course, to forgive him (Luke 17:3).

Paul advised that "you who are spiritual" should inform another of his fault (Gal. 6:1). The clear implication is that if someone else has a shoe of criticism that fits you, you should put it on gracefully.

Who is spiritual? "The fruit of the Spirit is love, joy, peace, long-suffering, kindness, goodness, faithfulness, gentleness, self-control" (Gal. 5:22-23).

Only if you react to someone else's faults "in the Spirit" should you point out their shortcomings. In other words, awareness of someone else's faults is first an occasion for personal soul-searching. When *your* heart is right, *then* seek to help someone else.

For the purpose of perfecting His people God has also ordained pastors, evangelists, and teachers (Eph. 4:11-12). One who clearly exhibits the marks of his God-given call cannot only help you see yourself, but help you grow into maturity as you deal with the truth you discover.

A Painful Process

It may be one thing for a person to say in apparent sincerity that he wants to know himself, but the experience of doing so is quite another. A revealing glimpse of yourself is seldom a welcome one.

If your self-image is to be meaningful, it must be measured against a standard. Here our premise is that regardless of the means to self-discovery, the Bible provides the standard. For example, if you find bitterness in your heart toward others, you must measure yourself against the biblical standard which states: "May the Lord make you increase and abound in love to one another and to all, just as we do to you" (1 Thes. 3:12).

Self-discovery can be painful. For this reason you will be tempted to shrink from it. Jesus saw this tendency in the Pharisees, and said they justified themselves before men (Luke 16:15). Another time He said that people love darkness rather than light because their deeds are evil (John 3:19). They prefer not to come to the light because the light exposes their sins.

Not only does a man try to hide his true self from others, but James warned that he may *deceive himself:* "Be doers of the Word, and not hearers only, *deceiving yourselves*" (James

1:22, italics added). Unfortunately, "Better to let sleeping dogs lie" is usually preferred to discovering yourself.

For Jack and Ann, discovering their true natures was indeed a painful process. They considered themselves sincere Christians—and they were. They believed they were devoted to one another and dedicated to a like-minded partnership—and they were. To them, their sincerity meant that if their objectives were askew, God would have revealed this to them. God *was* at work in their lives, but it did not seem like it—not with this thick wall of silence between them, or Ann's tears, or Jack's temper.

What caused the buildup of their "crisis"? To get the answer, each had to want to know the truth about himself. And so do you, to solve your problem. Ask yourself these questions:

- What am I really like?
- What does a pat on the back do for me?
- What does a rebuke do to me?
- What happens when I am crossed? mistreated? misunderstood?

As time went on, Jack gradually discovered that though he had given in to Ann consistently, there were deep-seated reservations in his heart and vague irritation over some of his decisions to go along with her logical arguments. He accepted her neatness and thrift and the pace she set for him in church activity. He accepted intellectually, that is—but not wholeheartedly. He was like the little boy who, when told by his father to sit down in the car, sat down but said that inside he was still standing up.

Jack's experiences with Ann brought him to discover himself. Conditions in his job confirmed his discovery. He realized he was doing the same thing there—conceding to well-reasoned propositions outwardly, but not inwardly. As the Apostle Paul put it: "Whatever you do, do it heartily, as to the Lord and not to men" (Col. 3:23).

Jack had strong opinions of his own, and did not readily accept the views of others. With friends he could drift in and out of associations, which he did frequently in an effort to be comfortable. But when he married, he could not trade his wife for another when she annoyed him. The result was a growing sense of dissatisfaction. Since he could not escape from this discomfort, he tried to isolate himself from it by building a wall between himself and Ann.

On that rainy day his dissatisfaction suddenly flared, and he himself was surprised by it. Fortunately, that shouting episode brought his problem into focus. He saw that he could not admit to himself that he was making concessions he did not want to make, even though he was agreeing verbally to what was reasonable, logical, and desirable. He had discovered his selfish nature.

But what was he to do with this discovery, or insight? He could deny or ignore it, and be like the man who looked at himself in the three-way mirror while buying a suit and was horrified by his double chin and bulging waist. The man's response from then on was to stay away from three-way mirrors. Jack could also admit the truth of his discovery, but confession would not have meant automatic correction.

Ann found out some things about herself too. She had had her own way most of the time, thanks to her ingenuity and power of persuasion. It was true that her standards were fine ones. But Ann was also a very determined woman. This trait showed itself when she insisted on a neat room in college, even if she had to do her roommate's share of the work. It was apparent in the way she kept after Jack to hang up his coat and put away his shoes. Perhaps instead of "determined," "stubborn" is a better word.

If Ann failed to win people over by logic, she broke into tears or lapsed into silence till her opponent gave in. Perhaps "sulk" is the proper word. Ann just couldn't or wouldn't back down.

Ann came to see this herself. What was she to do with this discovery? Now knowing her strengths and weaknesses, was she to manipulate them to further serve her own selfish ends? Or should she admit her stubborn nature with a view to changing?

If she chose to defend her emotional ups and downs, she had the Bible as the standard by which to determine whether her defense was valid. If, under the guidance of the Holy Spirit, she found she did not measure up to that standard, she had the grace of God available to change her.

Self-discovery is painful because it uncovers streaks in your makeup that you wish were not there—but which cannot be wished away. It confirms what John wrote almost 2,000 years ago: "If we say that we have no sin, we deceive ourselves" (1 John 1:8).

The objective is not morbid introspection, but an inward look for the purpose of moving on to higher ground. What causes me to be the way I am? I want to know because I don't want to live like this any longer. Other people have come to this conclusion about me a long time ago; it is about time I catch up with them.

Marriage, parenthood, a social situation, or your job may be the means to discovering your true self. But do not look for the root of your problem in your marriage partner or children or uncooperative neighbor; rather look for it in yourself. That which reveals a problem is not the problem itself. To treat the symptom is not to cure the disease.

A Helping Hand from Heaven

For a life of peace you must first discover your true self. Then to know what you have found, you must measure it by God's standard. You will find yourself short—everyone does. "For all have sinned and fall short of the glory of God" (Rom. 3:23). This is the reason you need the help which only Jesus Christ can give you. He alone can make you what you ought to be.

For Jack and Ann to change, they had to acknowledge their faults to themselves and one another, set aside their excuses, turn Godward, and truly seek forgiveness, cleansing, and spiritual strength on a daily basis. For Jack, he needed to admit that he only pretended agreement, deceived people, and hid an angry spirit. For Ann, she needed to admit her selfishness, stubbornness, and resentment. Because Jesus atoned for the sins of man at the Cross, God will forgive, cleanse, and give them new spirits.

Jack and Ann also had to move from verbal agreements to mental assent. As the Bible declares: "Now I plead with you, brethren, by the name of our Lord Jesus Christ, that you all speak the same thing, and that there be no divisions among you, but that you be perfectly joined together in the same mind and in the same judgment" (1 Cor. 1:10).

3
After Discovery— What?

What is your reaction when a friend confides, "I'm going to be very frank. There's something about you that I wish were not true"?

Do you grasp his hand and pull him to a chair so he can sit down and tell you your shortcoming? Do you fairly shout for joy that here is another glimpse of your true nature, that you are about to take the first step toward peace—self-discovery?

If he has a compliment, you are only too glad to have him say it; you don't even draw him apart from the crowd to hear it. But how hard it is to have your faults pointed out.

Much study has been given to the best ways of dealing with a person's faults. An often-used approach is to first give the person realistic praise in order to soften the criticism that follows. Dale Carnegie taught that if you want to win friends and influence people you should not criticize at all. He had a point. The average person resists facing up to his faults. Quite likely he will reject the person who points out his error.

Jesus Christ gave the precise explanation for this when He said: "For everyone practicing evil hates the light and does not come to the light, lest his deeds should be exposed" (John 3:20). Man possesses a natural dislike for rebuke. He has a built-in resistance to seeing his shortcomings.

We react to reproof as we react to pain. The tendency is to shrink away, to protect ourselves from what we wish were not so. James bluntly described our sinful nature in his epistle:

> But what about the feuds and struggles that exist among you—where do you suppose they come from? Can't you see that they arise from conflicting passions within yourselves? You crave for something and don't get it; you are murderously jealous of what others have got and which you can't possess yourselves; you struggle and fight with one another. You don't get what you want because you don't ask God for it. And when you do ask He doesn't give it to you, for you ask in quite the wrong spirit—you only want to satisfy your own desires (James 4:1-3, PH).

The Necessity of Reproof

Reproof, however, is good—like the surgeon's scalpel or the dentist's drill. The process is painful, but the result is health.

A man in our town suffered ill health for a year. He was one who didn't like to go to doctors; he was afraid they might tell him something he did not want to hear. When the man could no longer stand the pain, he visited a physician who informed him he suffered from a malignancy that would kill him within a few months.

"There might have been good hope for your recovery if you had come sooner," the doctor said.

This man had hated to face the truth. He believed that by denying he suffered or by ignoring the pain he somehow would get by. But he died—right on schedule.

In human relations it appears more sensible—at least easier—to ignore one's own fault or that of another. But the results are strained relations, strife, discord, and personal misery. A simple, effective alternative is, "If we walk in the light as He [God] is in the light, we have fellowship with one another, and the blood of Jesus Christ His Son cleanses us from all sin" (1 John 1:7).

A variety of sources will shed light on your pathway, primarily the Bible. King David said: "Your word is a lamp to my feet and a light to my path" (Ps. 119:105). The Apostle Paul wrote that "by the law is the knowledge of sin" (Rom. 3:20). Humanly speaking, when you step from darkness into light, your first impulse is to close your eyes or turn away. I have found that when we approach the Bible and it reproves us, the response is similar. One wants to turn away because the feeling is unpleasant. It was Jesus who commented about His own words:

> Heaven and earth will pass away, but My words will by no means pass away (Matt. 24:35).
> Blessed are those who hear the word of God and keep it (Luke 11:28).
> It is the Spirit who gives life; the flesh profits nothing. The words that I speak to you are spirit, and they are life (John 6:63).
> Sanctify them by Your truth. Your word is truth (John 17:17).

Studying the Bible is a sure way to get at the truth about yourself, but it takes some effort and no one can force you to study it.

The daily requirements of marriage, or the give-and-take situations that arise between college roommates, or the necessity for members of a committee or an athletic team to work in harmony, can likewise be immensely helpful to the individual who would get at the bottom of his problem.

Facing the Unpleasant Truth

As the truth about you emerges from some probing stimulus, you will either face it directly or turn from it. You will mellow or harden, depending on what you choose to do about your discovery.

A young couple stepped into the counseling room.

"How is it that at times we can be so cooperative, so tender toward each other, and 15 minutes later so opposed, so hostile, so cold?" asked Marvin, the husband. "How is it possible that we can pray together and feel united in our faith but when Sunday is past, or our time of morning devotions over, we don't even think of God and we battle each other?"

Marvin then opened the door on their lives to afford a glimpse inside. He remembered the day he and Gloria, his wife, had driven to the city hospital and parked. As they glanced up to the eighth floor, Marvin breathed a prayer for their three-year-old son who hovered there between life and death. "Dear God, we love our boy and we want him, but may Thy will be done. Help Gloria and me to be worthy parents and give Jimmy a happy home."

At that moment Marvin and Gloria felt closer to each other than at any time in their lives. Carefully he helped her out of the car; arm in arm they walked to the door and made their way up to the boy's room. Jimmy was asleep. A solution of some sort was being fed from a bottle into his arm. The parents looked at their son and their hearts beat as one for him. Marvin felt that he could never speak harshly to the boy again, that he could know no selfishness toward his son.

Jimmy recovered. What joy for Marvin and Gloria to bring him home! But after a week, the feelings Marvin experienced at the hospital had changed. In fact, antagonism toward both his wife and son crept into Marvin's heart.

The boy had been waited on night and day in the hospital. After he arrived home, Gloria kept up the pampering. This provoked Marvin.

"When are you going to let him grow up?" he asked his wife.

One evening Jimmy was playing on the floor near the sofa where his parents were reading. Insistently, he said his mother should go into the next room and fetch his favorite truck. She put down her magazine and started for the toy.

"Let him go for it himself, Gloria," Marvin said.

"I don't mind getting it for him," she replied.

Marvin nearly exploded. "You're spoiling him rotten! All he needs to do is point a finger and you jump."

Dad insisted that the boy get his own toy. The child begged and pleaded and began to whine. Gloria became increasingly uncomfortable. Finally she defied her husband and got the truck. Jimmy was happy, but his father was enraged.

After Jimmy went to bed, a silence developed between the parents. Marvin felt quite justified for having taken his stand. Gloria felt Marvin was being too strict. Whereas in the car outside the hospital and by their son's bedside they had shared the tenderest of feelings and identical goals, now they were distinctly opponents.

The associations of most people parallel at some time the fluctuating course in which Marvin and Gloria found themselves. The details vary, but the theme is the same. What father has not pledged himself to being a great dad and a wonderful husband and then has not found himself so angry at both his wife and children that he is capable of lashing out and hurting the very ones he loves?

The Bible describes this dilemma: "For what I am doing, I do not understand. For what I will to do, that I do not practice; but what I hate, that I do. Now if I do what I will not to do, it is no longer I who do it, but sin that dwells in me" (Rom. 7:15, 20).

What is it that keeps Marvin and Gloria from making good on their commitments to live consistently? They must be saved from themselves, just as the Apostle Paul wrote that the solution to his dilemma was outside of himself: "O wretched man that I am! Who will deliver me from this body of death? I thank God—through Jesus Christ our Lord! So then, with the mind I myself serve the law of God, but with the flesh the law of sin" (Rom. 7:24-25).

Any person who would hit the target of consistency must be saved from the drive within him that causes him to miss the mark. He must first discover and then face the truth about himself. He must realize that God alone is the One who can help him. John wrote in his first epistle:

> If we refuse to admit that we are sinners, then we live in a world of illusion and truth becomes a stranger to us. But if we freely admit that we have sinned, we find God utterly reliable and straightforward—He forgives our sins and makes us thoroughly clean from all that is evil. For if we take up the attitude, "we have not sinned," we flatly deny God's diagnosis of our condition and cut ourselves off from what He has to say to us (1 John 1:8-10, PH).

When this was brought to their attention, both Marvin and Gloria responded negatively. "Are you calling us sinners?" They found it hard to face the truth, even though they were fully aware that their behavior was inconsistent. They knew they both missed the mark that they had agreed to aim at.

How thoughtful and compassionate and generous we intend to be toward others in our relationships. Husbands and wives, or partners in a business, chart a course that each fully expects to follow. But somewhere along the way the trail is lost, one deviates from the path, and the target is missed. God says this waywardness is iniquity, or sin. "All we like sheep have gone astray; we have turned, every one, to his own way" (Isa. 53:6).

Yet who wants to agree that such failure is sin? Rather than face the truth, a person makes excuses: "I'm snappish today because I'm tired." "I spanked the child because his stubbornness makes me so mad I can hardly see straight."

Sin Stands in the Way

Marvin and Gloria left the counseling session, assuring each other of their devotion. They renewed their vows never to fall short again. But they were soon back. They couldn't inspire each other to be consistent.

"But we are Christians," they pleaded. "What can we do?" John wrote: "I write these things [which give you a true picture of yourself] . . . to help you to avoid sin. But if a man should sin, remember that our advocate before the Father is Jesus Christ the righteous, the One who made personal atonement for our sins" (1 John 2:1-2, PH).

You must be careful with the word "sin"; you must be sure of its meaning. Sin is the inability to do the good you want to do; it is the drive within you that causes you to do what you don't want to do (Rom. 7:14b-15, 19).

Marvin and Gloria have moments when both agree that they are violently opposed to each other. Yet when they try to face the truth, they deny it and attempt to reassure each other that all is well. But it isn't. They want peace, but they fight the process that leads to peace. They fail to take advantage of one of the important benefits of marriage—the means that marriage provides to self-discovery. Because the tendency is to fight against such discovery, many find marriage distasteful. They do not like to be reproved, even if the criticism is true.

The same holds true regarding work, social, and church relationships. The story of George Lund illustrates the point. George wanted to clear up the gnawing sense of anxiety and growing unhappiness that plagued him, hopefully before anyone found out his condition; so he sought professional counseling. He would rather have died than have his associates learn that he was bored with church and its activities, dissatisfied with his wife, and annoyed with his fellow employees at work.

But the counseling experience was a shattering one. The counselor, who George felt was a non-Christian, pressed him to share his antagonisms, and George did not like it. He insisted he had no antagonisms. He stoutly maintained that since he was a Christian he loved everyone and was nice to all. Still the counselor probed. Finally George blew his top.

Afterward he was ashamed. He had been a poor example of what a Christian ought to be. The counselor pointed out that George was filled with anger and hatred toward people, rather than with love.

Then George came to see me. He was confused. Was he a Christian or wasn't he? He had asked God to give him love toward all persons. Hadn't he meant it? "Since this counselor forced me to blow up," he said, "I've been pretty nasty to a lot of people." What evil thing, he wanted to know, had the counselor done to him?

What *had* the counselor done? He had led George to face the truth about himself. What truth? That he was an angry man with hatred burning in his heart toward the people with whom he worshiped at church, toward the people he worked alongside of at the office, toward his own wife and family—and now, toward the counselor, who, he maintained, had caused him to blow his top.

Because George pretended to be a happy man, he wanted to believe that he was one. That was why, since becoming a Christian, he had always acted politely to everyone. His annoyance was his own secret. He controlled himself for the sake of his testimony. The psalmist described such a man: "The words of his mouth were smoother than butter, but war was in his heart; his words were softer than oil, yet they were drawn swords" (Ps. 55:21).

Pretending to be happy didn't make him so. Yet he believed

that essentially he was a happy man. He was only being true to human form. "The heart is deceitful above all things, and desperately wicked; who can know it?" (Jer. 17:9)

George Lund's emotions—his heart—told him he was a nice, loving, happy man. But he refused to recognize the deceit of his heart. What the counselor had done was to expose George to himself, to lay open the falseness of his heart. He made George see that his smooth, soft words covered a bitter war raging inside, that they sheathed the swords of hate and malice.

George might have discovered this truth for himself. Like the fever that warns that all is not well in the body, the gnawing sense of uneasiness in his relationships with others ought to have made him aware that all was not well between him and the people in his life. But George did the natural thing—he disregarded the symptoms, denying the truth.

Because he was a Christian, George could not admit to himself that there was anything in his heart but love. And this is where Christians often encounter difficulty. Unlike non-Christians, who can despise others and unashamedly justify their position, Christians know they have a high and noble standard to measure up to. Non-Christians may settle for a less exacting standard. They know that if they fail, everyone else fails as much as they. So why not relax instead of trying to change the world? But for Christians, God's standard allows no bitterness and strife. Therefore, if they are not always what they know they should be, they at least *act* like Christians.

George was proud of his acting ability. "Usually I control my anger," he said. "Don't I get any credit for that?" His ability to *act* lovingly toward others presented an impressive testimony; but it did not satisfy him. As he became aware that he was only acting, the truth shook him up; he began to lose the control that he had so tightly held.

"I'm confused. Why doesn't God give me peace?" he asked.

Though the truth told him that he was only acting, he found it hard to admit it. How hard it is to help a self-righteous man! He sees no need to turn to God for help. But the Bible states that sin *does* lurk in the heart: "Your iniquities have separated you from your God; and your sins have hidden His face from you, so that He will not hear" (Isa. 59:2).

Repentance is rare. One tends to defend himself. Time after time George insisted he was an innocent man. He said the fault lay with the conduct of people around him, including the goad-ing counselor. Nevertheless, the facts of his case contradicted him. His iniquities separated him from God and denied him God's peace.

When he finally did focus on the true picture of himself, he became not repentant but defensive, dismissing his own re-sponsibility.

"He egged me on," George said repeatedly, reminding me that the flare-up was not his fault. One day he admitted that maybe he did lack love for certain people. But if he did, he asked petulantly, why didn't God give it to him? Now he blamed God for his anger.

When you get a glimpse of your true nature, it is to be expected that you will want to dodge the truth. But be aware that when you deny what you find in the recesses of your life, the results will be anxiousness and vague unhappiness that slowly envelop you in their tentacles.

Fifteen-year-old Gene described himself as easy to get along with. But he came for counseling because of his hair-trigger temper. He had been thrown off the football team for fighting. Once at home, his mother demanded that he study instead of going outside to play baseball. Gene became so incensed that he threw his ball through the picture window.

When I asked him about this display of temper, he dismissed any responsibility for it with a shrug. "Oh, I only get mad with my mother," he said. "Anybody would around her."

"What about the fights you get into at school?" I asked.

"Well, if you'd been in my place, you'd have punched them out too. Anyone with guts would have. You'd defend yourself, wouldn't you?"

Gene was a self-willed boy. He had no friends because they refused to put up with his lack of consideration and his quick fists. In spite of all the facts, Gene still insisted that he was an easygoing fellow. He really believed it; he was unhappy that others did not.

Fred Crompton came to my clinic because he was suffering from exhaustion. He was busy as a deacon in the church, made weekly calls on Sunday School absentees, served on the counseling team of the citywide youth rally, and headed the planning committee of the local Christian businessmen's organization. Fred hardly ever missed a meeting at church. He also played tennis once a week and faithfully followed his son's high school sports career.

Why wouldn't so active a man wear out? Yet his doctor could find no physical cause for his complaints.

In talking with him I learned that a year before, a trusted partner had cheated Fred out of his half of a business. I also learned that the demanding schedule Fred followed had started about the time of his loss. Fred had no explanation.

"I've got the time to do the things I've always wanted to do," he said. "I'm glad I can do them."

"You mean you are thankful that you lost the business?" I asked.

"I had committed the business to God," he replied. "The Lord gives and the Lord takes away."

"Were you as busy in the partnership as you are now?" I asked.

"Oh, busier. I was a workhorse."

"Did you get exhausted then?"

"Not at all."

"Now you aren't as busy as you were before, but you're on the verge of a mental and physical breakdown. How do you explain that?"

He couldn't.

I asked if he still had contact with the man who had cheated him. He replied that their paths crossed occasionally.

"We see each other. I hold no hard feelings at all toward him."

"What was your reaction toward him when you first learned that he had cheated you?" I inquired.

"Must we go into *that?*" he said, quite annoyed. "The incident is past. I have forgiven him. Let's forget it!" It seemed to me that Fred Crompton was getting hot under the collar. At least the flush of his skin indicated that he was certainly disturbed.

In later interviews it became clear that Fred was carrying a grudge against his former partner. He hated to admit it, but he was a deeply bitter man. Rather than face his reactions to an injustice, Fred had tried to bury them in a flurry of activity. Though he maintained a good front outwardly, the inward decay had pushed him to a point of near-collapse.

Stop Struggling—Come to Terms

The first step toward peace is to discover yourself. The second is to square up with the truth you find.

You will get fleeting glimpses of your true self (and sometimes a very clear picture) as you interact with other people, as you read the Bible, as the ministry of others touches your life. The natural reaction is to shrink away from your findings. Thus you struggle against yourself in your quest for peace.

But you need not run from yourself and thereby add trouble on trouble. The resources of heaven are yours to apply against the character defects you discover. Jesus died to forgive your sins: "In whom we have redemption through His blood, the forgiveness of sins" (Col. 1:14).

Furthermore, God will give you daily strength if you let Him: "Present yourselves to God as being alive from the dead, and your members as instruments of righteousness to God. For sin shall not have dominion over you, for you are not under law but under grace" (Rom. 6:13-14). "But now having been set free from sin, and having become slaves of God, you have your fruit to holiness, and the end, everlasting life" (Rom. 6:22). "The fruit of the Spirit is love, joy, peace, long-suffering, kindness, goodness, faithfulness, gentleness, self-control" (Gal. 5:22-23).

4
What Your Emotions Tell about You

The Carters were discussing a friend whom they admired. "He is such a cheerful person; you always find him in a good mood."

As they talked, the telephone rang. Mrs. Carter answered it; when she hung up she said to her husband, "That was Cliff Brown. Alice had her baby last night—a girl, just what they wanted. Cliff is walking on air."

In describing a person's response to life—your own or someone else's—you speak of feelings and emotions. When looked at objectively, these tell much about the person. In your own case you might well regard your emotions as guideposts on the route to self-discovery.

If your response to an unexpected change, a challenging idea, or just the daily routine is a positive one, you may use one or more of these words to describe your emotions: happy, cheerful, delighted, in high spirits, in a good mood, elated, thrilled, cordial, warm-hearted, enthusiastic, inspired, comfortable, glad, merry, pleased, joyful, overjoyed, gentle, affectionate, peaceful, long-suffering, meek, temperate, tender, forgiving, in accord, forbearing, genial.

But of course there is also a negative response. When in a good mood, Ted is a pleasant person to be around, but if you catch him when he's mad—look out!

"I can tell his mood by the way he shuts the door," his wife says. "If he nearly breaks the window in slamming it, I brace myself for his first gripe."

And come it will—followed by other complaints. "Why don't you make those kids keep their bicycles out of the driveway?" "Turn off that TV. There's racket enough around here without that thing adding to it!" "Women drivers! They should be kept off the highways after 3 in the afternoon!"

Negative responses such as these can cause much misery in life. Edward Strecker and Kenneth Appel have compiled a list of words that people use to describe anger:

> When the presence of anger is detected in a person we say he is mad, bitter, frustrated, griped, fed up, sore, hot under the collar, excited (now don't get excited), seething, annoyed, troubled, inflamed, indignant, antagonistic, exasperated, vexed, furious, provoked, hurt, irked, sick (she makes me sick), pained (he gives me a pain), cross, hostile, ferocious, savage, vicious, deadly, dangerous, offensive.
>
> Then, since anger is energy and impels individuals to do things intending to hurt or destroy, there is a whole series of verbs which depict actions motivated by anger: to hate, wound, damage, annihilate, despise, scorn, disdain, loathe, vilify, curse, despoil, ruin, demolish, abhor, abominate, desolate, ridicule, tease, kid, get even, laugh at, humiliate, goad, shame, criticize, cut, take out spite on, rail at, scold, bawl out, humble, irritate, beat up, take for a ride, ostracize, fight, beat, vanquish, compete with, brutalize, curse, offend, bully (*Discovering Ourselves,* Macmillan, pp. 114-115).

Emotions and Physical Change

Whether the emotion is positive or negative, pleasant or unpleasant, it produces physical changes in the body that are
familiar to everyone. The heartbeat increases; breaths are shor-
ter; muscles grow tense; digestion is affected; a person per-
spires and undergoes glandular changes that put him on the
alert.

Think what happens to a child when he becomes excited—
particularly when the excitement continues over a period of
time. Six-year-old John begged his father to take him to the
airport. One night his father said he would take him the next
day. How excited John became. After tossing in his sleep, he
was awake bright and early. He could hardly sit through school,
his body was so tense. He talked airport and airplanes to his
schoolmates, his teachers, the traffic officer on the corner, to
anyone who would listen.

About 5 that evening, he jumped up and down and clapped
his hands when he saw his father drive up.

"Dad's here! Dad's here!" He whipped out of the house to
the car. Before his father could get out, he asked, "We're still
going, aren't we, Dad? Aren't we?"

"Of course we're going," his dad replied. John ran back into
the house with a shout. He only picked at his supper. His body
did not require much food under the circumstances.

Jan looked forward to a date with the young man she thought
was the most popular in the entire school. All day long she was
keyed up. Her appetite disappeared. Even her memory became
faulty. Her mother had given her a chore to do that she forgot
about due to her excitement over the date. Neither could she
study.

The doorbell rang. She heard his voice. Her excitement was
at a high point. Her heart began to pound, her hands to sweat.
Her face flushed. Making a last check of makeup, she found
that her hands trembled. She experienced evident bodily changes
that brought a pleasant sensation.

Larry was elated. He had a date, doubling with a buddy and his girlfriend. He whistled and sang as he prepared to leave. His father had given him the car for the evening, and it had been no task at all to get it cleaned up for the occasion.

But when Larry drove in that night he was glum and disgusted. What had happened? His girl was late; the food bill was high; his friend and his friend's date got into an argument. The evening had been a flop. What a switch from the elation he had enjoyed as he was getting ready! His feelings had changed from pleasant to unpleasant, and so did his bodily functions.

You can easily see that emotions, whether pleasant or unpleasant, cause you to do something—jump up and down, sit and fret, pace the floor. The bodily changes, however, must return to normal for you to be comfortable and at ease. Where nature is not thwarted, this usually occurs with a minimum of effort. A child who has had an exciting day drops into his bed at night in sheer exhaustion.

With adults, letting nature take its course is often not so easily done. But returning to balance is no less essential for them than for children. Even the tenderest of emotions, pleasant as they are, must subside, allowing bodily processes to revert to normal.

Impelled to Act

The fact that an emotion may be pleasant does not make the quest for it desirable. The thrill of speed can be dangerous and deadly. The drive of sexual passion can throw you into deep trouble. Just the enjoyment of companionship can cause you to neglect important details and relationships in life.

It is the unpleasant emotions, however, that lead to the greatest troubles. The list by Strecker and Appel is unpleasant to read, but more so to experience. Unpleasant emotions impel you to act. In the case of anger, the impulse is to fight. The ultimate aim of fighting is to kill or destroy. Perhaps John had this in mind when he wrote: "Whoever hates his brother is a murderer" (1 John 3:15).

The difference between mild anger and murder is only a matter of degree. If you grant the truth of this, then you should consider anger and its related emotions as the deadliest cancers and treat them as such.

Of course it takes a lot of anger to carry out the impulse to harm someone. But who at some time has not thrown something in disgust? Watch two schoolboys fighting. Neither means to stop till he has vanquished the other. Look at the newspaper headlines and you see that angry nations, movements, and ideologies are engaged in deadly struggles. James warned, "Where envy and self-seeking exist, confusion and every evil thing will be there" (James 3:16). For the man who treasures envy and self-seeking in his heart, the impulse to hurt or to destroy is not far off.

Observe a child long enough and you will see demonstrated the angry heart. One day I was a guest in a home where a three-year-old boy lived. To entertain him while my hostess prepared dinner, I gave him my billfold to play with. When he started removing the cards, I took it back from him. But this young fellow was not the type to easily give up something he wanted. First he begged me to give it to him. Then he said he wouldn't like me if I did not do as he wished. Seeing that neither approach worked, he threw himself to the floor and kicked his feet up and down. This too failed to move me. He went off into another room and sulked.

Ruled by Wrath
Karl Menninger, the noted psychiatrist, says, "However sweetly we may interpret the fact, the human child usually begins his life in anger . . . the cry of the child just born has the tone not of lamentation, but of wrath" (*Love Against Hate*, Harcourt, Brace, and World, p. 9).

Many people never lose this natural tendency toward anger. Wayne Hartley was an angry man. He moved from job to job because "worldly people" irked him. Finally he landed at a firm with a Christian president. Here was a man he felt he could work for; he looked forward to a happy relationship on the job.

But things did not turn out that way. Hartley was made general manager, having a number of foremen to supervise. One of the foremen used a great deal of profanity. One day Hartley could stand his talk no longer, so he called him aside and ordered him to refrain. The foreman paid no attention. So Hartley warned him again, "Stop it—or you'll get fired!"

The company president heard of Hartley's ultimatum. He called his general manager in. "Joe's got a foul mouth, I know," the president said. "But he gets more work out of his crew than any of our other foremen."

He told Hartley to leave the man alone. Hartley was not to impose his private standards on Joe or any other employee. Reluctantly Hartley accepted the president's directive. But from that day on he felt he was constantly being overruled by the president. One day he stormed into the president's office, demanding a showdown.

"Am I the general manager or not?" he thundered.

"Why do you ask? Do you think you are the president?"

Wayne Hartley saw red. He shouted at his superior, waving his finger under his nose. He was completely angry—from the top of his head to the soles of his feet.

Telling of the incident later, Hartley said: "It takes a lot to get me mad, but when I am, the fur really flies. There we stood, toe to toe and nose to nose, yelling at each other. And both of us profess to be Christians. But you can be sure of this—no non-Christian ever made me more miserable than that man."

Did his boss cause Wayne Hartley to blow up?

"Who else?" Wayne demanded. "The last time he crossed me was the very last straw. I don't lose control of myself unless I'm forced to."

Here was a man who claimed to believe the Bible, which contains this verse: "God is able to make all grace abound toward you, that you always having all sufficiency in all things, have an abundance for every good work" (2 Cor. 9:8).

Could such grace be available to Wayne Hartley? Yes. First, however, he had to take an honest look at himself. When he did, he saw that he brought a spirit of antagonism to his new job. He didn't like to be crossed—whether by the foreman who violated his standard of speech or by the president who refused to let Wayne impose his standard on another. The frustration of not getting his own way exposed the wrath within him, just as frustration generally exposes the inner life of a man.

In looking back over his life, Wayne Hartley could see that he had possessed an antagonistic spirit since childhood. It had come out at home, at school, toward his wife, and his children, toward anyone who thwarted him. He did not blow up very often, but when he did, everyone got out of his way. He controlled things pretty well by simply threatening to blow up. At times, however, he met persons who just let him blow. This was true of the people he worked with; and this explained why he moved from job to job. By such moves he was able to dismiss his own problem, saying that his reasons for moving were the worldliness, selfishness, or cantankerousness of others. He always had a good reason for his tantrums.

The Bible says, "Be angry and do not sin; do not let the sun go down on your wrath" (Eph. 4:26). What was Wayne Hartley doing? He was accumulating wrath day after day. He even denied that he himself had anything to do with it.

His situation could be likened to a sink with a dripping faucet. Put the plug in and the sink fills up. The next drop will cause the water to run over. Is it the last drop that spills the water onto the floor? No, it's the last drop *plus* all the rest of the drops. Wayne Hartley had an irritable attitude toward life. Tiny irritations at home, at church, at work, on the way to and from work all slowly accumulated. At the same time pressure was increasing. Usually he could work off some of the pressure and drain away some of the irritation. But occasionally he was trapped; the last drop, or "the last straw," would cause him to blow up.

For a long time he could not admit that he was an angry man. Therefore he had no need, no occasion, to pray for forgiveness or grace. He needed none, he told himself.

"I get along fine unless someone else is unreasonable," he said. "And is it my fault if someone else is unreasonable?" Yet the Bible says, "Do not let the sun go down on *your* wrath" (italics added).

When Wayne Hartley accepted the fact that the wrath was in *him,* he found help in dealing with it. And that is the good news for everyone filled with anger and malice and bitterness. The people in your life may never change their ways. Circumstances may be beyond your control. But fortunately *you* can do something about yourself. You can open your heart to God, who is able to fill it with bountiful grace. But whether you allow God to give you His grace is your decision.

Strangely, most persons who seek counsel will argue that they have the right to be angry. "Under my circumstances, can you blame me?" they will say in stout defense. Of course they have the *right* to be angry, but as long as they argue in defense of their wrath, they will see no need nor have any desire to change and thus be delivered from the unhappiness of anger.

Sometimes a person can ignore his anger by becoming preoccupied with a problem. Lois Flood is a case in point. "When I get up to sing in church, my chest tightens and I struggle for breath. I am afraid I will fail. Lately I've been overcome with a sense of inferiority."

But she was not inferior. She was, in fact, the best vocalist in the community. What then was wrong? A look backward revealed the church in which she sang had a policy that soloists should rotate Sunday by Sunday—the lesser singers taking their turns with the better. This meant that Mrs. Flood had opportunity to sing only a few times each year. It annoyed her to listen to those who were far less competent than she. When she did sing, it was to people who angered her.

She had another problem. A circle in the church excluded her because of her age. Though she tried hard to be a member of the group, she was not accepted—only reminded that she belonged in another circle. So whenever she sang, she sang to women who angered her.

Lois Flood was not an inferior woman, but she *was* angry, bitter, and resentful. Day after day, week after week, the sun went down on her wrath. When she looked at herself honestly and faced the truth, she dealt not with feelings of being inferior but with her real problem—her selfish reactions to not getting her own way—and prayed for grace to accept what she could not change. She saw that up to this point she had had to give herself some reason for her uneasiness, and the reason she gave was, "I am inferior."

Feelings of Guilt

Anger receives a great deal of attention in mental health clinics and counseling centers all over the country. So do guilt feelings. A mother feels guilty because she screams at her children. A young man feels guilty because he no longer adheres to the behavioral standards by which he was reared. Another youth has been involved very intimately with a girl and feels guilty but cannot seem to help himself.

Some writers in the mental health field suggest that guilt feelings are the result of unreasonably high standards of conduct. People feel guilty because they are rejected or criticized. Therefore, they say, we need to accept one another as we are.

Commenting on this point, O. H. Mowrer, of the University of Illinois, says:

Our attitudes, as would-be therapists or helping persons, toward the neurotic are apparently less important than *his* attitude *toward himself,* [which] in the most general sense is a rejecting one. Therefore, we have reasoned, the way to get the neurotic to accept and love himself is for us to love and accept *him,* an inference which flows from the Freudian assumption that the patient is not really guilty or sinful but only fancies himself so . . . and that we are all inherently good and are corrupted by our experiences with the external world.

But what is here generally overlooked, it seems, is that recovery is most assuredly attained, not by helping a person reject and rise above his sins, but by helping him *accept them.*

This is the paradox which we have not at all understood and which is the very crux of the problem. Just so long as a person lives under the shadow of real, unacknowledged, and unexpiated guilt, he *cannot* (if he has any character at all) "accept himself"; and all *our* efforts to reassure him will avail nothing. He will continue to hate himself and to suffer the inevitable consequences of self-hatred. But the moment he (with or without assistance) begins to accept his guilt and his sinfulness, the possibility of radical reformation opens up; and with this, the individual may legitimately, though not without pain and effort, pass from deep, pervasive self-rejection and self-torture to a new freedom of self-respect and peace   ("Sin, the Lesser of Two Evils," *The American Psychologist,* May 1960, p. 303).

The mother who blames herself for losing her temper with her children and the young people who are ashamed of their conduct are not, Mowrer would point out, struggling with imaginary guilt. Their guilt is real. They will find no relief from it till they face the truth and accept their sins as their own.

But to say, "I am like that," is going only halfway. Admission leads nowhere unless it imples a desire to change. It must mean that the mother sincerely wants help with her temper and the young people with their conduct, and that they turn to God for the help.

How precise 1 John 1:9 is on this point: "If we confess our sins, He is faithful and just to forgive us our sins and to cleanse us from all unrighteousness." The man who confesses this way—having faith that God is able and willing to help him *and* having a desire for God's help—is well on the way to peace. The man who admits, "I'm like that," but does nothing about changing, will not find genuine inner peace. Nor will the man who denies responsibility for the wrong he knows he has done.

Freedom from Fear
Another malady that plagues many people is fear. Strecker and Appel maintain that the causes of anger and the causes of fear are identical. In the case of anger, something has already happened. In the case of fear, there is the prospect that something will happen. This view makes these Bible verses come alive: "For God has not given us a spirit of fear, but of power and of love and of a sound mind" (2 Tim. 1:7). "There is no fear in love; but perfect love casts out fear, because fear involves torment. But he who fears has not been made perfect in love" (1 John 4:18).

Again the key to freedom from fear is a backward look. Examine your reactions to people who may threaten you. Ask yourself, "Am I annoyed toward someone?"

Lloyd Sterling was filled with vague fears. "I drive my tractor all alone in a field and find myself gripped with fear. A cold sweat breaks out and I tremble all over."

A study of his life brought out the answer to his problem. He was racked by smoldering hatred. He and a neighbor had quarreled over who would maintain a fence. He and his wife kept up a running battle over the discipline of the children. He was bitter toward a brother who was a better farmer than he.

Why was he afraid? Because he might lash out at his neighbor and lose the respect of the people in the community. In an angry moment in the house he might harm the children or cause his wife to leave him. In his fierce competitiveness with his brother he might make a rash business decision that could ruin his own livelihood.

Lloyd Sterling had reason to be afraid. Most people do. But the loving person is not afraid. If no immediate explanation for fear can be established, an inward look is necessary. What James wrote in his epistle may apply: "Where envy and self-seeking exist, confusion and every evil thing will be there" (James 3:16).

One further comment by Strecker and Appel:

> Countless people at every corner unnecessarily deprive themselves not only of pleasure, but actual necessities in order to assuage the goading of a troubled conscience and fulfill a need for punishment. Feelings of unworthiness, of undeservedness, result at every hand in conspicuous neglect of health, comfort, and peace of mind.
>
> The man who, unprovoked, insults his best friend, the man who fails to show up at an important business conference, the girl who refuses an invitation to a party she would very much like to go to, the man who declines to propose to the girl he loves and remains unmarried, the woman who spends endless hours in unnecessary housekeeping drudgery "working her fingers to the bone," the brilliant man who

insists upon engaging in a petty, monotonous routine, a drab, colorless existence, people who seem to
court accidents, and have always a tale of hard luck,
those who repeatedly make plans which seem inevi-
tably to lead to failure—all may be motivated by
guilt, the need for punishment or self-directed anger.
Added to this are countless hours of sleepless worry,
or self-recrimination, self-accusation, bitter regret,
which also may be traced to the same sources
(*Discovering Ourselves,* p. 132).

Revealing What's Inside

Most people cause their own misery. Their guilt is not imaginary, but real. An inward look and a backward look can give
the reasons and point the way to peace of mind. Yet such
self-views are not easy to achieve. Man tends to flee from the
truth about himself: "Men loved darkness rather than light,
because their deeds were evil" (John 3:19).

When a man discovers hatred in his heart, he usually finds
other disorders as well. His personality may resemble an ice-
berg. Perhaps only jealousy shows, or envy, or temper. But
submerged are other disastrous emotions that deny him peace.
And one emotion can hardly be dealt with singly; every evil
deed must be exposed to the light. Yet to what surprising
lengths people will go to avoid discovering that which may be
"under their skins."

Some of these methods of avoiding what one discovers about
himself will be discussed in the next three chapters.

5
Bending the Truth

One Sunday evening after church Mrs. Arnold spotted the Bradleys and invited them to the house for coffee.

"We'd love to come," Mrs. Bradley said, "but we must get the children home and off to bed. Tomorrow is a school day and they've had a busy weekend. Maybe another time."

Mrs. Arnold was a loud, talkative woman; the Bradleys did not want to subject themselves to an hour with her. Mrs. Bradley's answer got them off the hook and did not hurt anyone's feelings.

On the way home that night Mr. Bradley agreed with his wife that she had handled the situation extremely well. They both believed that she had done a wholesome and constructive thing by turning down Mrs. Arnold's invitation without hurting her feelings. This "invented reason" reply to the invitation was, however, a cover-up for why they did not accept the offer. Their answer was nothing short of a lie.

In his letter to the Ephesians, the Apostle Paul explained that God had given the church various skilled people to help it grow up—like evangelists, pastors, and teachers. Because of their ministry, he reminded the Ephesians: "We should no longer be children, tossed to and fro and carried about with every wind of doctrine, by the trickery of men, in the cunning craftiness by which they lie in wait to deceive, but, *speaking the truth in love,* may grow up in all things into Him who is the head— Christ" (Eph. 4:14-15, italics added). He later reemphasized, "Putting away lying, each one speak truth with his neighbor" (Eph. 4:25).

With this biblical advice in mind, how should Mrs. Bradley respond to Mrs. Arnold? What options does she have? Is she to bluntly tell Mrs. Arnold she is too loud and talkative? How can she decline without lying? One option is to decline without comment: "No thanks, not tonight" or "No thanks, we prefer not to." If pressed for a reason she could respond, "I prefer not to give a reason" or "Someday I'll tell you."

Truth has a rugged hill to climb. It is natural to deceive. It's much simpler to tell a lie. The other person may be satisfied, but Mrs. Bradley must live with herself.

It's Wrong to Rationalize

Deception is so common and follows such well-defined patterns that the patterns can be described. Taken together they are called "mental mechanisms." One such pattern, *rationalization,* is a process whereby one justifies his conduct. By using it he gives himself good reasons for doing bad things. Lying, for example, can be called tact or diplomacy. Obviously, anyone ought to be tactfully or diplomatically or lovingly honest. But deception is a sin. It is easy to convince oneself that to do right is wrong, and to do wrong is right. Isaiah wrote, "Woe to those who call evil good, and good evil" (Isa. 5:20).

Who has not faced the desire to do something that his better self tells him is not right, but still does it anyway? An example is exceeding the speed limit.

"I'm late getting home and I don't want to worry my wife,"

a speeding driver will say. It is a good enough excuse. But looking squarely at the facts, few persons would accept his reasoning as valid for breaking the law.

Most persons are at least vaguely aware of inconsistencies in their lives. It is hard not to rationalize them. How difficult we find it to get down to reality and face conflicts, or to harmonize disagreements. We dislike being shown up, having our pride injured, or having our true selves exposed.

After the last of their children was married, the Gaylords sought counseling for Mrs. Gaylord's incurable loneliness. As we looked into their story, we found more than a yearning to be with the children. Mr. and Mrs. Gaylord were at war with each other.

They had been unfriendly toward one another for years, having a long series of unresolved conflicts between them. Because they found no companionship in each other, Mrs. Gaylord gave herself wholly to rearing the children and he buried himself in his work. The children provided the buffer zone that allowed them to live fairly peaceably under one roof. In the children they found a way to tolerate each other. They rationalized their solution so that each believed he was giving his all solely for the children.

Even when they sought help, they thought Mrs. Gaylord's problem was loneliness. Mr. Gaylord was very concerned. He said he would do anything to help her get over her loneliness.

Once they faced the real problem—their cold-war-turned-hot now that the children had taken away the buffer strip—they started to work on the solution. It was not easy. They had developed so strong a habit of camouflaging the truth that they needed a great amount of help in breaking out of their almost automatic pattern of self-deception.

As an example, for years he thought nothing of telephoning his wife to say that he had to take a customer out to dinner. The truth was, however, that he at times almost begged a customer to eat with him because he did not want to go home.

Rationalization can become a subtle habit of the inner life. Dishonesty and deception can in time become so easy to live with that you can "kid" yourself into believing whatever you want to believe.

We Deceive Ourselves
Charles Cook was anxious and restless. He found it hard to concentrate. When he sat down, he could never relax, so he got up frequently to pace the floor, to get a drink of water, to check the time, to look out the window. Cordial and friendly though, Charles was the type of person who made you feel that in him you really had someone who cared about you and your problems.

"Give me a call—anytime," he would sing out cheerfully to everyone visiting his office. Or, "You've got to come over to the house and tell me more about it."

Some persons took him up on his offers of hospitality. And there was the rub! His friendliness was an act. He didn't really mean for business associates to call him—let alone drop in at his home. He was just making conversation.

Whenever trapped, he had a way of getting out.

"I'd be glad to stop by some night," a client would say in response to his invitation. "How about Thursday?"

"Sounds fine. But let me check with the wife's plans and call you," Cook would say. Not for a minute did he intend to have this guy taking up *his* evening. The next day he would telephone the client to apologize.

"Sorry, but my wife's got me tied up with the PTA Thursday night. Let me contact you later."

Why did he invite people to call or visit him? It was the polite thing to do. Why did he then lie to the one he had invited? He did not want to hurt anyone's feelings.

But occasionally Charles Cook could not get out of his self-made trap. He would have to play the role of genial host to people he did not like. His acting was superb. But what a distasteful way of life! Is there any wonder that he was an anxious, uneasy man? "Bread gained by deceit is sweet to a man, but afterward his mouth will be filled with gravel" (Prov. 20:17).

Charles Cook imagined himself a cordial and polite individual because he sounded like one. But by his rationalization he was covering up a basic dislike of people and had fooled even himself into thinking he was a congenial man.

He needed to face the fact that his geniality was only a front. But to deceive even himself was easier than squaring up with the truth. Yet he could not get away with his duplicity. "For as he thinks in his heart, so is he" (Prov. 23:7).

Charles had to make up his mind what he wanted in life—whether to be around people or not. If he wanted to accept others, he would need a change of heart. Whatever his decision, if he was to be free of his anxiety, his behavior had to be changed to match the desire of his heart.

Bruce Hampton, a senior in college, had just gotten word that he would not graduate because he failed two subjects. He came close to passing in both, but narrowly missed the needed grades.

In both cases, the professors were known to be sticklers for utmost accuracy, allowing no leniency in their marking systems. Both were particularly hard on athletes—and Bruce had played four years of football and basketball. This was a simple retaliation, according to Bruce.

The fact was that 95 percent of the students in these classes passed and Bruce Hampton failed only because he neglected to study. But it is hard to say, "I seldom cracked a book and took my chances on passing or failing." It is natural to dodge the truth and come up with an excuse that sounds reasonable. As Sir Walter Scott once wrote, "Oh what a tangled web we weave, when first we practice to deceive."

Through rationalization it is possible to persuade yourself that an actual weakness of your character is a virtue. A white-hot temper can become, in your thinking, an instrument to produce righteousness in others. A real difficulty can be regarded as a big joke. Good deeds can be a mask for an appetite that thrives on praise. A spirit of revenge can be cast in the framework of a search for justice. You can make yourself appear better than you really are and by your effort mislead others.

Rationalization starts when you are unwilling to admit the unpleasant truth. Cheryl and Dave, just out of high school, were very much in love. Their parents said they were too young to get married. Dave ought to get more schooling, and Cheryl needed the maturation a job would bring. But the young couple saw the future differently.

He was a carryout boy at a supermarket. He didn't make much money, but they knew that somehow they'd get along on it. So despite the pleading of both sets of parents they were married. They found a dingy apartment in a part of town that neither was used to living in, gathered up some odds and ends of furniture, and began life together.

Theirs would be the most romantic of marriages. They would rise from rags to riches. Then in their third month of marriage Cheryl got pregnant.

How thrilled they were that soon they would be parents! But one day Dave came home from the store to find Cheryl crying. She had been crying most of the day. The dingy apartment depressed her.

Dave's heart was touched. He decided to surprise her. The next day he ordered a new electric stove. As if by magic, Cheryl was transformed into a radiant person. She enjoyed life again. But not for long.

The contrast between the new stove and the rest of the room was too much for her to take. So Dave went out and ordered a decorating job and more new kitchen equipment. She became happy again—for awhile.

When they came for counseling, they had a newly painted and papered apartment, all new furniture—and debts that had all but drowned them. And Dave had an unhappy wife again.

Both wanted to believe that their only problem was a matter of what their apartment looked like. On the basis of this rationalization they plunged in over their heads in debt. Their problem was much more involved.

Both were willful persons. They had paid no attention to the advice of their parents and friends who cautioned them not to enter marriage hastily. They simply were not able to afford marriage, but they had refused to look at this fact. They could not stand their tiny apartment on the wrong side of the tracks. Cheryl resented her pregnancy. He despised her cooking, having assumed that all girls could cook as well as his mother and finding out that she was the one great exception. Neither Dave nor Cheryl could even shop wisely. But they desperately sought to rationalize their problems by covering them with paint on the walls and a new rug on the floor.

Their unwillingness to recognize the root of their unhappiness and conflicts caused them to turn to self-deception, which led them into a new set of problems that was as frustrating as the old.

Both were basically selfish. When their wills coincided, there was no problem. But she demanded a nicer place to live. When she had to admit they could not afford it, she became difficult. He went into debt to avoid being the one to receive the brunt of her misery, but he resented having to do so. And all the time they told each other that if their parents would cut out the nagging and he could just make a little more money, they would be supremely happy.

Truth or Consequences

Deception violates a biblical standard. "Lying lips are an abomination to the Lord, but those who deal truthfully are His delight" (Prov. 12:22). "May the Lord cut off all flattering lips, and the tongue that speaks proud things" (Ps. 12:3). "We are meant to hold firmly to the truth in love, and to grow up in every way into Christ, the head" (Eph. 4:15, PH).

If you form the habit of ignoring facts, brushing aside the truth, making things come out to suit yourself, you will react in just these ways when a serious crisis comes into your life. You cannot rationalize the small decisions and then expect to make the major decisions in good, unfettered judgment. By practice you can become an expert at dodging issues or at facing them frankly and honestly.

The biblical standard of dealing only in truth is not designed to be a nuisance to the one who would abide by it. Rather it is the pathway to peace. Rationalization, on the other hand, will thwart your progress in life.

The key to inner peace is self-discovery. The method is to forsake the wrongs you discover. "He who covers his sins will not prosper, but whoever confesses and forsakes them will have mercy" (Prov. 28:13).

6
Other Faulty Patterns

Another "mental mechanism" or means of getting your own way is *regression*. To regress is simply to revert to childish ways of reacting to unpleasant situations.

How does a child get his own way? A couple in church were trying to keep their two-year-old quiet. The little fellow insisted on standing up in the pew, but his father wanted him to sit down. The boy slipped from the seat and started to crawl into the aisle. The father picked him up and forcibly held him on his lap. The child then let out a shriek; despite both parents' frantic efforts to quiet him he continued crying loudly. There was nothing to do but for the father to hurry out of the church with the boy.

The youngster won the round, even if it meant he would get a spanking. He wanted to get free from the confinement of the pew, and he did.

A child will resort to tears, screams, temper tantrums, or sulking to get his way. He will break things, fight, throw up, refuse to eat, or become generally hard to manage. He finds that such methods work amazingly well in getting what he wants. Because of past successes he is reluctant to give up his tried and proven means to an end.

But, as he grows, he learns that his childish techniques must be abandoned or at least restrained; he learns that other people have rights that must be respected. He discovers that to live happily, he must accept the fact that he cannot always satisfy his wants and desires. He learns, for example, that honor, respect, praise, and love come not from demand or by force but because they are earned by work, honest effort, and continuous adjustment to changing circumstances.

Childish Behavior by "Grown-ups"

The person who progresses steadily from childhood into adulthood shifts gradually and quite normally with the situations of life. Sometimes, however, a person will meet rebuffs, disappointments, failure, or tragedy with regressive behavior.

Janet Dean keeps an immaculate house—but her method is to "clam up" if someone walks across her carpet with dusty shoes. Her husband, who is not so fussy about how the house looks, has learned that he is better off if he spends his spare time tinkering with his tools in the basement instead of sitting in the living room. He doesn't want to run the risk of upsetting his wife.

Mrs. Dean rules the roost; she controls a big, strong, rugged man by the simple device of resorting to a childish form of behavior—pouting.

Jim Carver appears to be a placid man. But those who know him intimately are fully aware that if things go against his liking he will lose his temper. As his associates give in to his demands, it may appear that they agree with him. But all they are doing is preventing a nasty storm from developing. Hence, he controls a situation by merely threatening to regress to childish behavior.

A business executive came running down one of the long

corridors of Chicago's O'Hare International Airport. Breathlessly he approached the agent at the gate, presented his ticket, and inquired if his plane had departed. The agent shook his head; the executive was too late.

"That's my plane out there, isn't it?" he demanded, pointing to a jet on the concrete apron. Yes, it was his plane. But all preparations had been made for departure and the jet was beginning to taxi away from the boarding site.

"Maybe you don't know who I am," said the man. He was an important officer in a large corporation. The agent said he was sorry but there was nothing he could do. Then, with perhaps 100 persons looking on, the executive exploded.

"I warn you, if you don't get me on that plane I'll personally see that your airline suffers where it hurts—right in the pocketbook! And I'll see that you're the first to suffer."

The executive worked himself into a frenzy, embarrassing himself in front of the agent and spectators. But his blustering behavior did nothing for him—except to chip away at his own self-respect.

Sometimes regressive behavior works; sometimes it doesn't. But even when it succeeds in achieving an objective, it leaves the one who uses it with at least a vague disappointment in himself.

Many of the unhappy people who seek the help of a counselor are getting all they want; but they wake up to the fact that they are out on a limb alone thanks to their childish behavior. Other people avoid or ignore them. Some put up with them for the sake of politeness, or because they have something to gain for their tolerance.

Getting your own way by hysteria, by bullying, by vengeful silence, by cleverness and scheming does not give you contentment. Yet how often we attempt to get our own way by any means we think will work.

The Route to Maturity

Psychiatrists, psychologists, social workers, and personnel directors all agree that regressive behavior is a hindrance to wholesome relationships and a sense of self-respect. The Bible summarizes regression and its antidote in Ephesians 4:31-32. "Let all bitterness, wrath, anger, clamor, and evil speaking be put away from you, with all malice" (v. 31). Clearly this is a description of childish behavior with its excessive emotions and careless, hurtful expression.

"And be kind to one another, tenderhearted, forgiving one another, just as God in Christ also forgave you" (v. 32). This is an obvious description of a Christian who is "grown-up."

Most people who seek counseling say they want to be mature. They want to earn the honor, the admiration, the respect, the faith of others. Not all, however, are willing to recognize that to become such a person is to exercise reasonable self-control. Some are slow to learn the means of avoiding regression to childish behavior.

The Apostle Paul charted the route to maturity in writing to the Colossians. He told the Christians of that city to "put off" anger, wrath, malice, blasphemy, filthy communication, and not to "lie to one another" (Col. 3:8-9). In place of such behavior, he instructed them to "put on" mercy, kindness, humility, meekness, long-suffering, forbearance, and forgiveness (3:12-13).

"But above all these things," Paul continued, "put on love, which is the bond of perfection. And let the peace of God rule in your hearts, to which also you were called in one body; and be thankful" (3:14-15).

Suppression and Repression

Another mechanism that a person may use to achieve his ends is *suppression*. In literature on psychology, suppression is referred to as a conscious, deliberate, purposeful forgetting or submerging of unpleasant childhood experiences and negative reactions to people and circumstances.

To illustrate: Archie Rudd's father was a demanding, dominating, cruel man. He required Archie to perform a long list of chores letter-perfect. If the boy slipped up or stepped out of line, his dad lashed out at him with severe verbal whippings. Sometimes he required a form of penance, such as writing a thousand times, "I will never again disobey my father."

Archie grew up hating his father. As an adult he repressed the memory of his childhood most of the time. When someone gave him a direct order, however, he saw the image of his father in that person and reacted negatively to him.

Suppression is not limited to experiences of the distant past. Most persons have at some time had the desire to cut down an opponent with a searing remark. Men often confess during counseling that they must exercise great control to keep from hitting their wives. Occasionally, a mother will tell how she must shake off an urge to inflict physical harm on a disobedient child, perhaps with the knife she is using to pare potatoes. In the growing-up process everyone has known what it is to have desires, emotions, and natural inclinations that are at variance with the demands of society. Unfortunately, the usual way of dealing with nonpermissible thoughts is to relegate them to the back of your mind.

Repression also involves submerging or forgetting unhappy past experiences, negative attitudes, aspirations, or feelings. It differs from suppression in that by repression the unhappy experiences or attitudes *are not* pushed out of the mind *knowingly.*

One's collection of gripes, complaints, hates, and suppressed desires and actions can become so great that many of them disappear from memory. Though they no longer come to mind, they are nevertheless there. The fact that they lurk in the shadows is evident by frequent eruptions in the form of touchiness or anxiety. One becomes tense, irritable, uneasy, subject to long silences, sensitive, tired for no explainable reason, full of aches and pains that cannot be corrected by medical treatment. It is obvious that a person who is always in danger of being "upset" or "disturbed" can hardly have a peaceful mind or feel in tune with the people around him. Such persons are not only subject to "upsets" but are in danger of "breakdowns."

Over the last several years many psychologists have warned of the harm in repression. Some have said that a child should be allowed to grow up as he pleases. If left to himself, he will arrive at a way of life that makes him a happy person and an asset to society. Such management of children, however, has only illustrated the truth of the Bible's warning, "A child left to himself brings shame to his mother" (Prov. 29:15).

In the same verse is a statement that to some people is indeed strange, "The rod and reproof give wisdom." The wheel of child-rearing turns constantly. Current literature suggests the cycle is drawing near the biblical viewpoint: We *do* need a standard to go by.

Repression would be a wonderful way of escaping if simply forgetting a problem actually removed it. But such is not the case. Harsh, bitter, unforgiving emotions and attitudes are stored up, not eliminated, as long as they remain harsh, bitter, and unforgiving. Every so often something happens that springs open the trapdoor to the dark attic of the mind, and the negative things we thought we had forgotten come rushing out to cause misery to ourselves and others.

If suppression and repression fail as approaches to the harsh realities of life, what does work?

The Bible offers the answer: "Judge not, and you shall not be judged. Condemn not, and you shall not be condemned. Forgive, and you will be forgiven" (Luke 6:37). It is possible for you to look on the behavior of others and on their treatment of you in a noncondemning, forgiving spirit. To do so is not to whitewash the evils toward you, but to have an attitude toward spiteful persons that will free you from their hurt.

What about the guilt and remorse that stem from memories of the past? Recognition of your sins need not cause you anxiety, for on the heels of recognition is forgiveness and to be forgiven is to find release. "In whom [Jesus Christ] we have redemption through His blood, the forgiveness of sins" (Col. 1:14).

Other Ways to Cope

Other ways people seek to cope with the pressures that build up within them can only be touched on here.

Extroversion. The extrovert is a person who flees into a constant round of activity in the community, church, club, or place of employment. He is always on the go, always talking, always planning—using activity as a refuge from personal conflict. One person, however, should not judge another's motives. You may think you can distinguish between the one who serves and the one who is merely fleeing from his problems. But you may be completely wrong.

Introversion. The introvert builds a wall around himself. His world is entirely his own. One cannot easily learn his thoughts, desires, plans, dreams, or reactions. Many a man or woman would do well to withdraw from the crowd for serious thinking, to weigh and consider before acting. But this is not what the introvert is doing. He is not pondering in order to make a wise move. He is dodging issues, avoiding decisions, hiding from the world. He is enclosed in his own private supply of thoughts and dreams that will likely never happen.

Compartmental thinking. In a sense, this approach to conflict is to not let the right hand know what the left is doing. An example of this is the man who as a board member is careful to see that the church constitution is upheld, but who will take a drink with a customer, despite the church constitution, because to do so is good business. He will not drink socially because it is against his religious convictions; but business is business. Also in this category is the meticulously neat dresser whose house is an unbelievable mess.

Projection. This is a subtle form of self-deception in which one sees his own faults as belonging to someone or something else. He is the person who has a long list of complaints about his church associates, but who is very sure that the people don't like him. He is the one who is always on the edge of keeping the law but who becomes very critical of lawless people. He is the person who has a secret and in guarding it thinks that everyone is looking at him suspiciously or is talking about him.

The Alternative—Spirit-Filled Living
As one studies the mechanisms used to get around the truth, the accuracy of the Bible's description of man's heart as "deceitful" and "desperately wicked" (Jer. 17:9) becomes apparent. Thus, you need a resource outside yourself. The qualities that come from God will keep you from faulty handling of truth. They can be yours if you let Jesus Christ implant them in your life. The spiritual man is renewed day by day . . .
In comfort and consolation:

> Blessed be the God and Father of our Lord Jesus Christ, the Father of mercies and God of all comfort, who comforts us all in our tribulation, that we may be able to comfort those who are in any trouble, with the comfort with which we ourselves are comforted (2 Cor. 1:3-4).

In patience and joy:

> Strengthened with all might, according to His glorious power, for all patience and long-suffering with joy (Col. 1:11).

In wisdom:

> If any of you lacks wisdom, let him ask of God, who gives to all liberally and without reproach, and it will be given to him (James 1:5).

In righteousness:

> And be found in Him, not having my own righteousness, which is from the law, but that which is through faith in Christ, the righteousness which is from God by faith (Phil. 3:9).

In peace and hope:

> Now may the God of hope fill you with all joy and peace in believing, that you may abound in hope by the power of the Holy Spirit (Rom. 15:13).

7
Mind and Body

The body, host to the mind, can influence its invisible guest. I was reminded of this when traveling with a missionary friend in Africa several years ago. He was stricken with an attack of malaria. Over several days this normally keen individual was frequently delirious. At such times it was impossible for me to discuss anything of a serious nature with him.

Most persons need a given amount of sleep or they become irritable. Induction of a narcotic or alcohol into the body decreases the ability to think straight. Even food can affect the mental process—ask any luncheon speaker who has seen part of his audience drift off to sleep.

Though the body can influence the mind and one's emotional state, medical science avers that the mind holds even greater mastery over the body.

One day I encountered a highway accident just after it had happened. Three badly battered bodies lay motionless on the pavement. A survivor simply sat on the roadway and stared unseeingly at those who had been members of his family. Another who had lived through the crash stood beside the overturned car and screamed, "I killed them! I killed them! They told me to slow down. Why didn't I listen?"

I walked away from that scene literally sick to my stomach. In driving off I noticed that the muscles in my arms and legs were tense. I sighed frequently. My body had undergone distinct changes that were the result of my reaction to that bloody scene.

One day during counseling Charles Reed spoke of his problem at home. Often he would arrive home in a good mood and would be hungry enough to eat a side of beef. Then his wife would begin to air her complaints. Perhaps he had slammed the door when he had come in. Or he might have been a few minutes late. So just before dinner was ready, his body would become tense and he would lose his appetite. His reaction to his wife produced drastic bodily changes.

A young girl reported she suffered from severe headaches. Investigation disclosed they always occurred when her fiancé failed to call when he said he would. A further look back through her life showed that her headaches started about the time something went wrong with her plans.

Eddie Bond sought counseling at the recommendation of his physician. "How can *you* help me get over a stiff neck?" he asked, truly puzzled. As he told his story, it became clear that life was to him one big pain in the neck. The tenseness of his neck muscles gave him the pain. He was tense because he approached the problems in his life as if he were a football lineman charging his opponent.

Mrs. Frick was a beautiful, cultured, well-educated woman. But in certain situations she was having difficulty swallowing her food, until I learned that these times of difficulty came in connection with appointments that her husband demanded that she make and keep. She resented his demands. She actually could not "swallow" them.

The Body under Stress

Think of the common expressions that unite mind and body:

- My heart was in my mouth.
- I was so frightened I nearly jumped out of my skin.
- I was scared stiff.
- He makes my blood run cold.
- I was shocked.

These expressions indicate the relationship that exists between the mental/emotional state of a person and the workings of his body. For a better understanding of how this relationship functions, we must turn to the physician.

O. Spurgeon English, chairman of the Department of Psychiatry at the Temple University School of Medicine, speaks from long study of this relationship between mind and body. He tells us that there are certain emotional centers in the brain that are linked to the entire body through the autonomic nervous system. He describes charges of emotions that are relayed from the brain, down the spinal cord, and through the autonomic nerves to the blood vessels, muscle tissues, mucous membranes, and skin.

Under emotional stress, he points out, all parts of the body can be subject to physical discomfort because of a change in blood nourishment, glandular function, or muscle tone (*The Autonomic Nervous System,* Sandoz Pharmaceuticals).

You may have wondered, *How can thoughts and feelings going through my mind cause pain in some part of my body far from my brain?* Dr. English explains: An emotion such as fear can cause the mouth to become dry. This means that the blood vessels have constricted and the blood supply and glandular activity have been reduced. This dryness will occur, for example, in someone who must make a speech and is afraid.

Laboratory tests show that under emotional stress the same decrease in glandular activity occurs in the mucous membrane and various parts of the digestive tract. Not only does the blood

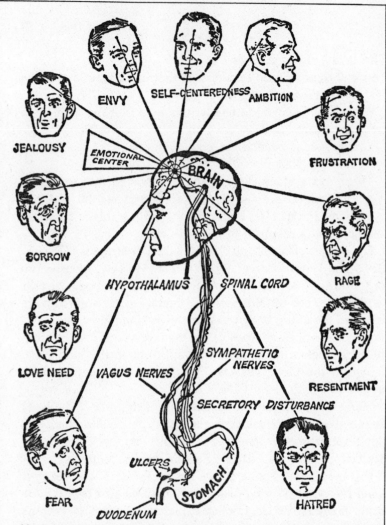

Various emotions which have their source in the brain find their way through definite pathways to the stomach. When a troublesome person can't be coped with, we say we can't "stomach" him—and that may be literally true. O. Spurgeon English, chairman of the Department of Psychiatry at the Temple University School of Medicine, points out that a poorly functioning personality can be the reason for disorders of the digestive tract. (Drawing used by permission of O. Spurgeon English.)

supply change markedly, but secretions of various types increase or decrease in an abnormal manner. Changes in muscle tone in the digestive region can occur, causing painful cramps.

It has also been proven that emotional stress will increase the size of the blood vessels in the head: this change in turn produces pain because of the stretching of the tissues around the blood vessels and their pressure on the nerve endings.

Of the heart, Dr. English says:

> Without the presence of any heart disease whatever, psychosomatic patients are prone to increased heart rate, irregularities of rhythm, unusual sensations about the heart such as oppression, tightening, pain, and numbness sometimes accompanied by shortness of breath and the feeling of faintness and weakness, possibly giddiness. Along with this so-called "spell" there may be a general "all-gone" feeling, free perspiration, accompanied by a sinking sensation and the feeling as if the patient would fall in a heap (*Psychosomatic Disorders of the Heart,* Sandoz Pharmaceuticals).

Joe Johnson collapsed at work and was rushed to a hospital, apparently a heart attack victim. But he had been having some social problems. For one thing, he and his wife were experiencing acute troubles. Then a neighbor acquired a dog that barked all night. Soon a promotion put him under more pressure. The last straw was the need to provide housing for his elderly parents. Why did he collapse? Because he was not adjusting happily to his life situation.

Dr. English points out that a poorly functioning personality can be the reason for psychosomatic disorders of the digestive tract:

For decades it has been known that a personality problem which cannot be solved by the mind itself is prone to be "turned over" or "taken up" by some other part of the body. When an irritating friend or a troublesome family member cannot be coped with, the patient becomes "sick," he can't "stomach" it, or it "gripes" him. The physician knows that the cause of these gastrointestinal disturbances is emotional conflict. He knows it is the attitudes of generosity and responsibility struggling with an opposing wish to escape them (*The Emotional Cause of Symptoms,* Sandoz Pharmaceuticals).

His description of the conflict within a person is surprisingly like the one the Apostle Paul presented in Galatians 5:17, PH): "For the whole energy of the lower nature is set against the Spirit, while the whole power of the Spirit is contrary to the lower nature. Here is the conflict, and that is why you are not free to do what you want to do." The physician and the Bible describe the same problem—the struggle between what ought to be done and the contrary wish to evade it.

The physical effects of this conflict are often referred to as "nerves." "My nerves are shot," a woman says. "I'm on edge," explains another person.

Just what is meant by a "nervous disorder"?

The human nervous system may be compared to a large telephone network. Through sensory nerves the brain, like a central telephone exchange, receives messages or sensations; through motor nerves, orders or impulses are sent out to the muscles so that action may be executed.

Consider the effect of a pistol shot. The sound waves enter the ear, then travel as sensory impulses to the brain and then to the muscles in the arms and legs, to the heart, lungs and intestines, resulting in a rapid heartbeat, increased rate of breathing, and alterations in the functioning of the intestines. The nervous system did not *cause* the fright, but served to alert the body to a sudden change that hinted of danger.

The Works of the Flesh and You

In describing the emotions that cause psychosomatic illnesses, the Bible and Dr. English describe similar emotions which cause psychosomatic illnesses. Compare the physician's list with God's:

Dr. English	The Bible
hatred	hatred
resentment	quarreling
rage	jealousy
frustration	bad temper
ambition	rivalry
self-centeredness	factions
envy	party spirit
jealousy	envy
sorrow	
love-need	
fear	

The emotions which English recognizes as being disease-producing are the same emotions that the Apostle Paul denounces and associates with man's "lower nature" (*Phillips*) or "flesh" (*New King James Version*). In either case, the words describe reactions to someone or something that gets in your way. Such reactions are not pleasant to acknowledge in one's life, particularly when they are tagged "the lower nature" or "works of the flesh." So the individual tends to deny their presence and perhaps deceives even himself. He focuses his attention not on the shameful reaction but on the bodily ailment that the reaction produces through his nervous and glandular systems.

Actual organic disease of the nervous system is easily observable under the microscope. Structural changes can be seen. But a case of "nerves" is something else.

If you have a viral infection in a nerve, you feel pain and tenderness along the course of the nerve. If you sever a main nerve running to a muscle, you are unable to move the muscle. But a "nervous" person has no physical impairment.

There is, then, the strange situation in which, on one hand, a person has a disease of the nerves without being "nervous" and, on the other hand, a person who speaks of being "nervous" but who has an apparently normal nervous system. The complaints of the "nervous" person are usually lodged in his stomach or intestines or heart—organs that are not a part of the nervous system.

Tom Fischer drove several hundred miles to reach our clinic. He came because he had stomach pains that the physicians said were functional. "That means," he said with a wincing grin and a report from the Mayo Clinic fresh in memory, "that my stomach pains are all in my head."

Essentially he was right about the term "functional," which means that the pain of an affected area is not caused by a disease. It also usually implies that the individual is not meeting his emotional problems in a wholesome way.

"They asked me if I was having any problems," he said. "What's that have to do with my stomach?"

When we first started talking, the idea of his getting well by talking to a counselor seemed a big joke. But he took the experience well—at least, he was getting a nice trip out of it.

But life to Tom Fischer was no joke. Especially his employment. Two events of several months ago were still "grinding" him. First, he had been transferred from one machine to another and he did not like the change. Then a company safety officer came along and ordered him to wear safety glasses. Tom refused, saying, "I never will." The company left it up to him—wear the glasses or quit. He ate his words.

As we talked, he became upset over his work situation. It was hard for him to admit it, but he hated his work, his boss, and the safety officer. He literally burned within. Then slowly he became more preoccupied with the pains that began to come than with the hate that had brought them on. He was learning to live with a distasteful work situation, though not liking it. As far as his stomach was concerned, he was sure cancer was eating it up.

Strecker and Appel describe a man like Fischer:

> Human beings stand a *single* mental shock relatively well, even if it is severe, like the drowning of an only son. It is a series of shocks or a long-continued emotional strain like worry or apprehension that finally breaks us. Such tiring and destructive emotional stress may be due to a prolonged struggle with difficulties and problems which we are not meeting in a straightforward manner. Long drawn-out fear, anger, shame, resentment, or other intense emotion may produce an increased heart rate and alterations in the activity of the gastrointestinal functions. If these reflexes are established, they tend to keep on going, even after the original situation has disappeared. Thus anxiety, states of intense fear, worry, agitation, and loss of control dominate every waking hour (*Discovering Ourselves,* Macmillan, p. 197).

This was Tom Fischer's problem—a long-term, slow burn of hate that switched to a preoccupation with his body. Tom said his physician called it nervous exhaustion, resulting from mental cross-purposes. With Fischer, it came because he was defeated by a personal problem. He held grudges against his boss and the safety officer. He, of course, could not express his resentment openly and keep his job, so he hid it. But in the effort, he became alert to every muscular pain as well as the sensations of heart and stomach functions. The interesting thing was that he could switch from the anguished details of his suffering to a cheerful, animated discussion of his trip. Turn the conversation back to his work—Tom Fischer would again begin to grimace. "I didn't realize how much I hate those men," he finally said.

How Hatred Destroys
S. I. McMillen, a physician skillful in writing as well as in practicing medicine, speaks of the devastating effects of hatred:

> The moment I start hating a man, I become his slave. I can't enjoy my work anymore because he even controls my thoughts. My resentments produce too many stress hormones in my body and I become fatigued after only a few hours of work. The work I formerly enjoyed is now drudgery. Even vacations cease to give me pleasure. It may be a luxurious car that I drive along a lake fringed with the autumnal beauty of maple, oak, and birch. As far as my experience of pleasure is concerned, I might as well be driving a wagon in mud and rain.
>
> The man I hate hounds me wherever I go. I can't escape his tyrannical grasp on my mind. When the waiter serves me porterhouse steak with french fries, asparagus, crisp salad, and strawberry shortcake smothered with ice cream, it might as well be stale bread and water. My teeth chew the food and I swallow it, but the man I hate will not permit me to enjoy it. . . .
>
> The man I hate may be many miles from my bedroom; but more cruel than any slave driver, he whips

my thoughts into such a frenzy that my innerspring mattress becomes a rack of torture. The lowliest of the serfs can sleep, but not I. I really must acknowledge the fact that I am a slave to every man on whom I pour the vials of my wrath (*None of These Diseases*, Revell, pp. 73-74).

Fortunately, the Bible points the way to a cure: "Let there be no more resentment, no more anger or temper, no more violent self-assertiveness, no more slander, and no more malicious remarks. Be kind to one another; be understanding. Be as ready to forgive others as God for Christ's sake has forgiven you" (Eph. 4:31-32, PH).

Strecker and Appel have an additional comment on the relationship of emotions to the body:

If aroused to a high pitch, shame, distress, hate, envy, jealousy all strike to the very core of our being. They leave us worn, tired, incapable, and almost helpless. The blush of shame, the haggard countenance of distress, the consuming burning of jealousy and envy, and the facial and vocal expressions of hate are striking testimonials to the deteriorating effect of these emotions upon the body. We may jump with joy or droop with sorrow (*Discovering Ourselves*, p. 12).

Like Dr. English, Strecker and Appel use practically the same words to describe hurtful emotions as the Bible does in speaking of the works of the flesh.

Reacting Biblically
S. I. McMillen says the stress of living does not cause big or little problems to adversely affect the body. Rather, it is one's *reactions* to his problems. Stress can be beneficial. It is the spirit of retaliation that calls forth glandular toxins.

"Is it not a remarkable fact," he asks, "that our reactions to stress determine whether stress is going to cure us or make us sick? Here is an important key to longer and happier living. We hold the key and can decide whether stress is going to work *for* us or *against* us. Our attitude decides whether stress makes us 'better or bitter' " (*None of These Diseases,* p. 111).

"Nervous" patients demand the kind of medicine that comes in a box or bottle. But they fail to recognize, say Strecker and Appel, that the medicine they need is mental peace. "It is almost axiomatic that in the presence of a clear, honest, and conscious understanding of the conflict, a neurosis cannot occur" (*Discovering Ourselves,* p. 204).

The Bible's admonition is to confess your lower nature or works of the flesh, your hurtful emotions—your sins—and God will be faithful to forgive your sins and to cleanse you from all unrighteousness (1 John 1:9). Admit to God that these things are true of you, and then cleansing—fellowship with the Lord and inner peace—will be yours.

The refreshing cleansing that comes from God is capable of washing away all aches and pains brought on by a troubled mind.

8
Positive Aspects of the Negative

Our description of man has led us into a gloomy pit. How difficult we find it to face the truth we have uncovered! As we look up, however, a comforting shaft of light pierces the darkness. It is the promised way of escape.

But before observing this way of escape, let us take one more look around.

There is a reason why so many people are unhappy, why there is so much conflict between individuals. Isaiah pinpointed the trouble long ago: "We have turned, every one, to his own way" (Isa. 53:6).

You like your own ideas, plans, aspirations, and longings. So does everyone else. Thus when a man encounters resistance to his wishes, or faces demands that are not to his liking, he tends to rebel, to attack, to run, or to defend himself. His natural reaction is to be resentful, bitter, stubborn, full of fight. It is easy for a person to think that his own desires are the reasonable ones. He will find a way to make a selfish drive seem selfless, deceiving even himself.

Furthermore, it is natural to shrink away from a glimpse of

oneself. To back off from reproof is as human as shielding the eyes from a burst of light in a dark room. Again, Jeremiah's assessment of the heart, that it is deceitful above all things (Jer. 17:9), and Jesus' statement that men love darkness rather than light because their deeds are evil (John 3:19) are as up-to-date as the literature on psychology that describes the mental mechanics for evading the truth.

The patterns of deceit and self-defense are so systematized that their names are common dictionary words. We have considered rationalization, regression, suppression, repression, extroversion, introversion, compartmental thinking, and projection—some of the more common ways of turning from the truth about oneself. To peer further into the darkness, such avenues can lead to psychoses requiring hospitalization—or to broken homes, crime, vice, or even murder or suicide.

Such is the heart of man. One shudders to contemplate its potential for evil. The Bible and literature on psychology alike paint this oppressive picture.

Scripture's Accurate Diagnosis

But, as already mentioned, there is hope. Since in this presentation we are looking to the Bible as our guide, we can turn to it not only for a description of man as he naturally is, but for the path away from our disturbances, neuroses, and psychoses and to peace.

"Great peace have those who love Your law, and nothing causes them to stumble," said the psalmist in Psalm 119:165. Is this possible?

Many persons turn to a counselor for help because they are in circumstances that offend them or have caused them to stumble. They are dissatisfied, irritated, unhappy. Either they flee from the vexing situation or attack it. One would think that people would rush to buy a book that pointed out the path to peace and freedom from offense. People *do* buy it. By the millions every year. The Bible continues to be the all-time bestseller. But it is a Book that most persons quickly lay aside.

Though man's hope lies in God and His Word, many people quickly turn aside from the Bible because it reproves and corrects. Man simply does not like the truth about himself that he finds in God's Word.

Churches are criticized because their ministers upset people when they preach about the sinfulness of man and the inflexible standards of the Bible. Once I had a long conversation with a fellow counselor about the value of "deeper life" conferences, in which the details of the ideal Christian life are discussed. He felt very strongly against this type of conference. He believed it did irreparable damage because after such a conference a wave of very upset people came to him. That they could not attain perfection greatly disturbed them.

People have often turned to me as a counselor because their pastor has upset them. Having listened to him preach about sin, they feel guilty and inadequate. As they relate the details of their stories, it invariably turns out that they were much happier people before they began attending church and studying the Bible. Therefore, could it not be reasonable to conclude that their problems were caused by what they heard and read? To remove the cause would seem to relieve the person's anxiety. And this has long been advocated. There is widespread pressure on ministers to preach "positive" messages and to emphasize the good in man.

Wait just a minute, though. Perhaps a look at the methods of other professions may help you understand the value of pointing out the "bad," the evil, the negative.

Consider the dentist's approach. Recently my dentist examined my teeth. He chatted amiably throughout the examination. He took some X rays. I can still see him holding his picture up to the light and saying, "There is a cavity, and there is one, and there is another. You have three cavities." How negative can you get? He did not even mention the good teeth.

Then he prepared to stick a long needle into my gums—not a pleasant experience at all. The drilling was no picnic either. In fact, there is nothing about going to a dentist that I like. It makes me a bit anxious to think about going, and decidedly annoyed when his bill comes. But yet we all go to the dentist. We respect this man who subjects us only to discomfort. Why? Surely not because of the process. The results are what we want. He could give us medicine that would cut the pain of a decaying tooth and make us feel comfortable as long as its effect remained. But unless the dentist got to the source of the problem, the decay would continue, and someday the pain would be even worse.

Consider the physician. As he diagnoses you, he has only one basic question: "What is wrong?" This is certainly a "negative" approach!

If 99 percent of you is in good health, your doctor is interested in only the 1 percent of you that is not. If you have an infected fingernail and the rest of you is healthy, he concentrates on the fingernail. If you have a pain in your abdomen, he does not overlook the abdomen. Instead he examines it thoroughly, even if the examination brings you pain.

Why do you put up with such treatment? Because his objective is to restore your health. He eliminates pain and may save you from death by subjecting you to great pain and even the risk of your life on the operating table. It is positive to eliminate the negative. It is healthy to eliminate disease. It is good to eliminate evil.

A neighbor in apparent good health went to her physician because she developed a slight pain. Investigation revealed a tumor and abdominal surgery was called for. The doctor's announcement of what was needed not only upset the woman, but her whole family and some people in the neighborhood as well. Why would a man want to subject this fine woman to such an ordeal? Why didn't he give her a sedative to help her forget the pain? No one would have gotten upset. But instead of prescribing a painkiller, he sent her off to a hospital, where her surgery confined her for five weeks.

Think of the effect of his diagnosis and prescription on the woman's husband, their children, their budget. But not a single person condemned the doctor. Quite the contrary, they were all grateful to him. They were appreciative of this person who had delivered such drastic, disturbing news and who had subjected her to the pain of a knife and her husband to such great expense. He would have done her a disservice to have acted otherwise.

Another thought on this subject: The diagnosis did not depend on the notions of the physician, but on the condition of the patient's body. He could not be guided by what the patient wanted to hear; rather he had to follow the course of his findings. How does one make the announcement of the need for major surgery a happy occasion? There is no way. The important thing is that the proper diagnosis be made and the patient be told. The patient will get over the shock of the announcement. My neighbor did. Then it was up to her whether she would submit to the prescribed treatment. She could have tried to ignore the pain, kept busy, and attempted to forget about her condition. She might have tried to kill the pain with medicine. Her other alternative was to accept surgery, which she did.

An accurate diagnosis of a physical ailment is a matter for the physician. But the patient's future health is really his own decision.

To miss the mark of perfect health is common, but to deny that one is sick when he is, or to give up the quest for health, is foolish. Wisdom calls for trying to discover the cause of ill health, for the physician to give an accurate diagnosis despite the guilt, anxiety, or worry it might cause, and for the patient, for his own best interest, to follow through on the doctor's advice.

Now back to the point that ministers are pressured to emphasize the "good" and the "positive" because talk of sin and the negatve is upsetting and causes anxiety and worry. Of course the knowledge of sin produces such results. But the immediate comfort of a person is of little value if there is, in fact, sin in the person's life. To diagnose sin, however disturbing it may be, is a positive act.

The minister, counselor, or friend cannot determine what the diagnosis will be. I cannot determine what my client brings to me. If there is selfishness, touchiness, irritability, stubbornness, rebellion, hate, or deceit within the person, it simply is there. I didn't put it there, but it is my responsibility to point out its presence. This may be upsetting. But I have found no other way. I have never known a person to discover the sin that is causing his trouble by my dwelling on his good qualities. And I have never found a way of pointing out a man's sin to him that makes him clap his hands with glee at the news. Jesus Christ emphasized this when He said of sinners: "But you are not willing to come to Me that you may have life" (John 5:40).

Jesus also explained why people feel condemned and guilty: "This is the condemnation, that light has come into the world, and men loved darkness rather than light because their deeds were evil" (John 3:19). This is why people become disturbed when they hear a minister of the Gospel preach on God's standards for man. The Bible throws light on their conduct; it exposes their souls. The truth is often offensive.

Once, after Jesus had addressed the Pharisees, His disciples said to Him: "Do You know that the Pharisees were offended when they heard this saying?" (Matt. 15:12)

What had offended them? This is part of what the Lord told them:

> Not what goes into the mouth defiles a man; but what comes out of the mouth, this defiles a man (Matt. 15:11).

Those things which proceed out of the mouth come
from the heart, and they defile the man (Matt. 15:18).

For out of the heart proceed evil thoughts, murders, adulteries, fornications, thefts, false witness,
blasphemies. These are the things which defile a man
(Matt. 15:19-20).

Though the words of Christ offended His listeners, their
response did not change the truth He spoke. And herein lies
tremendous hope. You may not be able to control what your
wife or husband, father or mother, or anyone else does, and
you may not be able to change your environment. But you
don't need to, because the real source of your problem is not
the people around you or your environment, but *you.* The
things that defile you come from within *you.* And this, in a
sense, is good news because *you* can be changed. But *you*
must decide whether to let God change you.

The Battle with the Will
To come to the decision that will lead you into the pleasant
valleys of peace is to struggle with your own will. To illustrate,
note the experience of Jerome Weller.

Weller was department foreman of a manufacturing firm in
Trenton, New Jersey. One day his boss called him into the
office and said, "Jerry, as you know, things are a bit slow
around here these days. I realize you have worked hard and run
one of the best departments in the company. But my orders
are to cut one supervisor, so I am letting you go."

Weller was stunned. He was the only Christian among the
foremen. The other supervisory personnel, including his boss,
liked to go out drinking and had some pretty wild parties
together. As a result, their work sometimes suffered and Jerry
had to step in to rescue them. He had worked hard. This was
his reward.

Weller now faced a financial slump. He had been making payments on a new home and a car. When his salary was suddenly cut off, he was in trouble. He lost both house and car and had to move in with his parents, who lived in Michigan. While with them, he had nothing to do but sit in a comfortable chair and mull over his experience.

So this is the reward for hard work and clean living, he would say to himself over and over. The more he thought, the more bitter he became. He found it hard to eat, harder to digest what little he did eat. He suffered from painful cramps. His physician told him that his condition stemmed from his emotions. But most of his friends reassured him that he had a right to have some emotional problems.

Twelve years later, time seemed to have healed the wound. Weller found another job and at this point was quite successful in it. He was, in fact, general manager of a manufacturing outfit with eight plants. One day while he was inspecting one of the plants, the personnel director asked him if he would like to meet the plant's new chief engineer. Of course he would, and did. Weller found himself face-to-face with the man who fired him 12 years before. Here working for him was the person who had caused him so much grief, pain, and embarrassment.

"I sure made a terrible mistake back there," the engineer said to Weller when they were alone. "Will you forgive me?"

"Oh, certainly. Forget it," Weller replied.

Jerome Weller said he would forgive, but within himself he nursed a gnawing bitterness toward this man. His stomach-ache returned. He began reliving those confusing, awful days of long ago. He had thought this period of his life was long forgotten, but he found himself fuming in his plush office, wanting only to get even.

One day he related the experience to me, then asked how one could work with a person who had treated him as this man had treated him.

What would have been your reply?

God's Enabling Power

I pointed out several Scripture passages to Jerome Weller. One was 2 Corinthians 4:7-10:

> But we have this treasure in earthen vessels, that the excellence of the power may be of God and not of us. We are hard pressed on every side, yet not crushed; we are perplexed, but not in despair; persecuted, but not forsaken; struck down, but not destroyed—always carrying about in the body the dying of the Lord Jesus, that the life of Jesus also may be manifested in our body.

The Apostle Paul spoke here of trouble, perplexity, persecution, rejection. All these had happened to this man. But Paul also said there is a power that will enable a man to face such treatment without distress, despair, self-pity, or ruin. It is the power of God. I discussed this with Jerry Weller, but at the time it seemed to mean little to him. I spoke of the end products of distress, pointing out that definite bodily changes are involved. Blood pressure, respiration, digestion can be affected, I said. Freedom from distress means that the body will function normally. But his body was upset.

"Are you suggesting that I am my own problem?" he asked. "Are you saying that you would have acted differently had you taken what I took?"

I assured him he was his own problem. Then I reminded him of one of Jesus' statements: "I say to you, love your enemies, bless those who curse you, do good to those who hate you, and pray for those who spitefully use you and persecute you" (Matt. 5:44). This, I said, should be his attitude toward the man who had fired him.   .

Weller became furious with me. How could I be so lacking in sympathy and understanding? Now he was upset not only at the engineer, but at me as well.

Who was this man hurting when he carried his grudge around within himself. Who was affected when he sat in his chair in Michigan and seethed over a man who lived 700 miles away? Obviously, he was hurting only himself. Who is hurt when you get upset over someone who isn't even in your presence? You, of course.

There is a power that will enable you to face your circum-stances without distress. It is the power of God, made available to you through the dying of the Lord Jesus. God's power—and His alone—can make you want to forgive one who has misused you. But Jerome Weller did not want to forgive that engineer. He wanted to get even.

He argued that he had a right to be bitter. I agreed he did and would agree with anyone who stoutly stood on his right to be angry and unforgiving over a wrong done to him. It is your privilege to be upset, to be miserable. As long as you insist on retaining your misery, you will have it.

The knowledge of sin, however, does not eliminate it or the problems that sin causes. Wise is the man who heeds the advice of the Apostle James:

> Be doers of the Word, and not hearers only, deceiving yourselves. For if anyone is a hearer of the Word and not a doer, he is like a man observing his natural face in a mirror; for he observes himself, goes away, and immediately forgets what kind of man he was (James 1:22-24).

The exhortation here is to those who want to be free from their misery, who want to be lifted out of their sin. But wasn't it strange that my counselee who said he wanted relief from his upset condition became all the more upset because I told him he did not need to be upset? One would think he would have seized the opportunity to shed his spirit of bitterness and hate. But that's not man's nature.

For many persons, to yield bitterness and hatred in exchange for a tender heart toward someone who doesn't deserve it would not be blessed relief, but great sacrifice. Like the general manager, untold numbers of persons would like to be free from their aches and pains, but if to be rid of them means to relinquish a long-standing grudge, they would rather ache.

There in his walnut-paneled, softly lit office we were locked in a struggle. If I had told him that his grudge was normal and that probably I would have acted the same way, he might have enjoyed some relief, but the inner sore would have continued to fester and spread its poison.

Willing to Yield

It is a mystery how a man finally quits fighting and turns to God for a spirit of love toward someone who does not deserve it. All we know is that there is generally a struggle before a man yields.

But when he does yield, his problem is nearly over. The Bible says it is *your* move. "Come to Me, all you who labor and are heavy laden, and I will give you rest" (Matt. 11:28).

One day, Jerry Weller did turn Godward for help. Today his digestive disorder is over, his aches and pains are gone. He is at peace with himself and with the man who had abused him. Jerry is enjoying God's peace, the fruit of the Spirit, in his life.

How does this change come about? By confessing or acknowledging that you have done wrong, that you have sinned. David wrote this about his sin: "I acknowledged my sin to You, and my iniquity I have not hidden. I said, 'I will confess my transgressions to the Lord,' and You forgave the iniquity of my sin" (Ps. 32:5).

When Weller paid attention to *his own reaction* to the other man's sins, instead of concerning himself with the man's sins, he found himself on the road to peace.

To see your sin is disturbing only if you fight what you discover. If, instead, you admit it and seek help from God, the result is not guilt but an overwhelming sense of forgiveness, cleansing, renewal, and peace.

The pathway to spiritual peace is a struggle. Discover the truth about yourself and you will naturally shrink from it; become offended and defensive and you will be bound in the strong fetters of your sin.

But what a difference you will find if you heed the promise of Jesus: "If you abide in My word, you are My disciples indeed. And you shall know the truth, and the truth shall make you free" (John 8:31b-32).

9
The Responsibility Is Yours

What is the key to mental health? How do you achieve and maintain peace of mind? Must you be at the mercy of your circumstances? Is it inevitable that a chance meeting can plunge you into the depths of despair?

Jerome Weller was a happy, successful man—he thought. Then by meeting someone he hadn't seen for 12 years he was, as if by magic, transported backward in time. Even though he sat at his expensive desk in his plush office, with the words "General Manager" on his door and several secretaries at his call, in his mind he was back in Trenton, a bitter, sweating, aching, confused young man who had been fired as the reward for working hard and living a clean life. He was reliving those days in which he lost his car and house and underwent the humiliating experience of moving in with his parents because he was broke. Sitting there now in air-conditioned comfort, this man who ran eight plants and directed the work of hundreds of men had only one thought—*revenge.*

But the Bible commands, "Repay no one evil for evil. Have

regard for good things in the sight of all men. If it is possible, as much as depends on you, live peaceably with all men. Beloved, do not avenge yourselves, but rather give place to wrath; for it is written, 'Vengeance is Mine; I will repay,' says the Lord" (Rom. 12:17-19).

Mr. Weller knew about these verses. We had also discussed Jesus' words: "Love your enemies, bless those who curse you, do good to those who hate you, and pray for those who spitefully use you and persecute you" (Matt. 5:44).

Were these thoughts a challenge to Mr. Weller? Not at first. They were in the Bible, to be sure, and Mr. Weller was a sincere and consistent Bible student. But right at that time these ideas were most unpalatable. To fire his old opponent was a thought that gave him much pleasure. Revenge, vengeance, evil for evil. Success, a plush office, money, power—these had not changed his vengeful heart.

He had nearly forgotten the lean years more than a decade ago. But now they came flooding back, and he had to choose— forgive or retaliate. The decision was up to him. It was *his reaction* to the past that would tip the balance.

He could not control some of the events of his life. He was the victim of someone's decision 12 years before, no question of that. Now it appeared he was again a victim, this time of a personnel director's decision to hire the one who had wronged him. Suddenly, there the man was, and successful, happy Mr. Weller was plunged into the depths of bitterness and hate.

It appears that circumstances and people dictated Mr. Weller's problem. But *he* was the one who did the reacting. His problem was *within* himself. Would he forgive or get even? It was obvious that the decision to retaliate would not be the key to his peace of mind. Since we know the outcome of his case, we recognize that the key to peace was his receiving from the Lord the power to forgive.

Peacemakers or Flame Fanners?

Mr. Weller illustrates the struggle men go through to find peace. Bitterness, hatred, and revenge are natural responses to troublesome people and events. But how much better it is to think in terms of making peace, rather than planning someone's destruction. Christ said: "Blessed are the peacemakers, for they shall be called sons of God" (Matt. 5:9).

Who would think Mr. Weller weak if he forgave the engineer who had wronged him? To forgive is a mark of maturity. And spiritual maturity brings peace, as the psalmist indicated: "Mark the blameless [mature] man, and observe the upright; for the future of that man is peace" (Ps. 37:37).

Do not avenge yourselves; live peaceably with all men; love, bless, forgive. These words place the responsibility for your decision squarely on your own shoulders. This is the essence of good mental health—*it depends on you.* You reap the results of your own decisions, your own reactions.

To get out of the gloomy pit of despair, bitterness, hostility, jealousy, and the accompanying aches, pains, and misery, you must take personal responsibility for your own character, no matter what someone else does—or did. If a man is miserable, it is his choice. His woe is not the result of his background, or the people around him, or his environment, but of a choice, either deliberate or vague, to continue in the direction that he has been heading.

Mr. Weller could have chosen either to forgive or to seek revenge. His misery or peace was due to his choice, which came from within, just as sickness is within a man. A person may have caught cold because he entered the company of persons who had colds. The reason for his cold can be explained. But since he caught a cold, he must be treated for his own cold, no matter how he got it.

So it is with unhappiness. No matter the origin (and the unhappy person can usually explain how he got that way), it is now his responsibility and his alone to take proper steps to correct the condition that is causing his unhappiness. But it should be mentioned here that understanding alone, without changing one's course, is a dead-end street.

Answerable for Our Actions

We cannot overemphasize: Man is miserable when he does not take responsibility for his own inner life, his own reactions and behavior toward the people and circumstances that come his way.

Jesus stated an obvious truth, "In the world you will have tribulation" (John 16:33). We all have our share of trouble and always will. But the presence of trouble does not alter personal responsibility. "For it is written: 'As I live, says the Lord, every knee shall bow to Me, and every tongue shall confess to God.' So then each of us shall give account of *himself* to God" (Rom. 14:11-12, italics added). Also, "For we must all appear before the judgment seat of Christ, that each one may receive the things done in the body, according to what he has done, whether good or bad" (2 Cor. 5:10).

Being either clearly or vaguely aware that we are answerable for our own conduct, is it any wonder that more and more people become miserable as they forsake biblical principles?

The Bible contains the guidelines that told Mr. Weller what his reaction should be *to* the people and events of his life. It also contains the guidelines that tell him what he ought to *do* about the people in his life. For example, Paul spoke plainly about our responsibility to others when he said that no Christian should "put a stumbling block or a cause to fall in . . . [his] brother's way" (Rom. 14:13).

Jesus said: "It is impossible that no offenses should come, but woe to him through whom they do come! It would be better for him if a millstone were hung around his neck and he were thrown into the sea, than that he should offend one of these little ones" (Luke 17:1-2). Again Jesus said: "Just as you want men to do to you, you also do to them likewise. But if you love those who love you, what credit is that to you? For even sinners love those who love them" (Luke 6:31-32).

The struggle for inner peace, as far as Jerome Weller was concerned, centered in his *reactions* to the engineer and in his decision about what he would *do* about him. When he accepted these responsibilities, he was well on the way to peace because he was then in step with what the Bible commands.

What good news it was that he could have inner peace if he wanted it, that the decisions were his own to make. He need not be a helpless victim of people and events. He himself determined whether or not he would have peace of mind and heart.

How Does Our Past Shape Us?

"Are you ruling out past history as the cause of a person's behavior?" you may ask.

There does appear to be a basis for assuming that past history shapes you. In counseling I generally find that the unhappy person who has been rejected rejects others; the victim of mean, angry, hateful people is also mean, angry, and hateful; the person who grew up in an atmosphere of suspicion is suspicious of others. People seem to reproduce in them-selves what they are exposed to.

We would agree that a man's circumstances seem to rub off on him, thereby giving him cause for happiness or discomfort. There is the mark of his parents, experiences with brothers and sisters, relationships gained through church and school activi-ties. He is the product of his family's economic status, his education, his body, his talents, his opportunities.

People who are unhappy have been mistreated. A woman who is withdrawn and sullen often has a mother who was withdrawn and sullen. People appear to be caught up in a circle, a vicious one, forged by generation after generation of example.

Harry and Val Adams were seriously at odds with one another. Among other things, they fought over the issue of going to church. Val insisted that they go for the sake of the children. Harry flatly refused.

"My father was a mean, selfish, two-faced man," he said. "Yet he was looked on at church as a saint. He made us go to church twice on Sunday and every Wednesday. 'But for what?' we kids always wanted to know.

"Sometimes my father and mother would get into a violent argument at the dinner table—less than an hour after dismissal of the Sunday School in which they both taught classes. I vowed that I would abandon church as soon as I got out on my own, and I'm sticking to my word."

As a boy, this man had witnessed some frightening conflicts between his parents. Here he was, carrying on similar quarrels with his wife. The subject was different, but the spirit was the same. He was as inconsiderate of his wife as his father had been of his mother. Despite his protests otherwise, Harry didn't go to church because he didn't want to go—not because of his father.

I once counseled a woman who was extremely "nervous." Her spells came on whenever her husband or children ignored her wishes. In short, she was a selfish woman. She had been pampered and spoiled all her life. Her explanation: "I was raised this way. Can I help it if I have this kind of personality?"

Another woman, recalling her past, remembered how frustrated and angry she became as a child because her mother refused to help her button up her jacket. "I would always end up with an extra buttonhole on top and a button at the bottom," she said. "Ever since, I have gotten mad when people force me to do something. My husband insists that I put his vitamin pill on his plate for breakfast and I just rebel at this. He can do it just as well himself."

This woman sees red if anyone crosses her, all because she was "buttoned up wrong," or so she believes. She takes no responsibility for her fiery temper. She dismisses it with a shrug, "It's the way I am. My husband knows it, and I get upset if I'm pushed."

These people do reflect their backgrounds. Harry Adams was like his father. The woman who was pampered and spoiled was just like her mother. The other, the one who was "buttoned up wrong," came from a home where tempers flared when anyone was crossed.

It is true that a child tends to absorb the atmosphere in which he was raised. It is also true that people tend to keep on going in the direction in which they are headed. But the Bible says, "You are inexcusable, O man, whoever you are who judge, for in whatever you judge another you condemn yourself; for you who judge practice the same things" (Rom. 2:1).

An unhappy person must come to terms with the people in his past, forgive them, and seek to understand the effect they have had on him. But this Bible verse says he has no grounds for reproducing the pattern, once he understands it.

There are happy, contented people who are considerate of others and who also have had difficult pasts. They too have been mistreated and rejected. But they have come to terms with their pasts, forgiving people who did not deserve forgiveness, charting their future courses as persons responsible for their own conduct. They have not produced the kinds of lives they have been exposed to.

Society's Cop-out

Ours is a land with plenty of good food, the best in educational opportunity, excellent transportation, the finest medical care. Yet in the midst of all this, we have a growing number of emotionally disturbed, unhappy, miserable people. Why?

Part of the answer comes in a recently reported interview

with Marvin A. Block, widely recognized authority on problem drinking. Dr. Block said that tolerance of drunken behavior has given impetus to consumption of alcohol in the United States. In the areas where drunkenness is not tolerated, there is little alcoholism. But where the control is lax, alcoholism flourishes. He added that people start using alcohol for relaxation and relief from the cares of the day.

This means that in our day it is socially acceptable to turn to a sedative rather than learn to adjust to life. When a man becomes addicted to liquor, we call him sick, and say that he has a disease—a medical problem. Yet behind this diagnosis is a person who must turn to alcohol to gain his relaxation and to escape from the strain of daily life. Professor O. H. Mowrer uses the term "dis-ease."

We regard the poorly adjusted person the same way we do the alcoholic. We say he is not responsible because he is nervous, maladjusted, upset. He has a personality problem. He suffers from a poor background. We make a medical problem out of his case. There is nothing about his malady that we can see by X ray or microscope, no germ or virus that the laboratory can detect. But we still call him sick.

How can you expect anything of someone who is sick? This man who is at odds with society and at war with himself must be nursed, favored, carefully handled. What is the result? We tend to reject personal responsibility for our conduct. But the fact of it remains.

To Follow or Not to Follow

Responsibility for your own conduct is illustrated in the area of physical health. The medical books explain the laws of good health. If you don't want to be tired, you must get enough sleep. If you wish to control your weight, you must not eat large quantities of certain foods. Often these rules interfere with your plans. You may have too many interesting things to do to make time for enough sleep. You may like mashed pota-toes covered with gravy, and a pie à la mode too much to push away from the table.

Whether you follow the rules is your choice. The medical books did not create your problem of tiredness or overweight. They only provide the description. It is futile for you to com-plain about such rigid rules. They may upset you, or cause you to suffer, but the physician cannot repeal them. He can only state them.

"Why am I built so that I must get so much sleep and eat properly?" you may demand to know. "I want to change the rules."

Can you eliminate your problem by ignoring the laws? Of course not. The man who transgresses the law of sleep is tired; the one who disobeys the rules of proper diet is overweight. Granted there may be other causes of fatigue and being over-weight; when these are present, the medical books will help you discover them. But if the medical books do not make a man tired or fat, neither does the Bible create anxieties and frustrations by setting a standard for living. It only describes the standard.

Why must we live by it? The rules are so upsetting you'd like to change them. But the Bible warns: "Do not be deceived, God is not mocked; for whatever a man sows, that he will also reap. For he who sows to his flesh will of the flesh reap corruption, but he who sows to the Spirit will of the Spirit reap everlasting life" (Gal. 6:7-8).

You can enjoy a full life and a lavish table of food. The process will give you much pleasure. But expect a tired and overweight body. You can ignore the principles of biblical liv-ing and enjoy yourself, but don't be surprised at the anxiety, tension, worry, unhappiness, conflict, or misery. We have not freed ourselves and found a life of ease and relaxation by writing off the Bible.

But, you say, there are other causes of these painful symptoms. Of course there are. Your physician can help you discover if there are medical problems involved. These can be corrected by medical means. If the symptoms remain, however, then consider a return to a way of life that is charted in the Bible.

The Bible tells us that we are responsible for the way we treat others and for our own attitudes and conduct. You may be tempted to neglect your health because of the people around you. But you, not they, will suffer illness if you do. You may have been mistreated in the past and are greatly tempted to hate, to rebel, to refuse to forgive, to insist on your own way, but it will be *you* who will be miserable and at cross-purposes with others.

Transgression of God's laws is called *sin* (1 John 3:4). This word need not disturb us. It simply means that you have violated some divine principles of spiritual living, just as the word *sick* means you have disobeyed some medical rules of physical living. You may not have been aware of the rules, but the results of your transgression do not take into account your ignorance. Any amount of reassurance of your innocence will not change the results.

Why are people uneasy? Turn again to the Bible:

> The wicked are like the troubled sea, when it cannot rest, whose waters cast up mire and dirt. "There is no peace," says my God, "for the wicked" (Isa. 57:20-21).
>
> The wicked flee when no man pursues; but the righteous are bold as a lion (Prov. 28:1).
>
> He who covers his sins will not prosper, but whoever confesses and forsakes them will have mercy (Prov. 28:13).
>
> Salvation is far from the wicked, for they do not seek Your statutes (Ps. 119:155).

It is personal sin, or wickedness as the Bible often calls it, that causes a man his misery, not the unrighteousness of someone else.

We are no more free to chart our own course for mental health than we are to lay out the road to physical health. No one condemns a man who gets sick because he unknowingly exposed himself to disease or was unaware that he had violated the rules of good health. But we are less sympathetic and call him foolish if he deliberately risks sickness. No one would condemn a man because he was exposed to mean and hateful treatment. But deliberate violation of biblical principles is another matter.

There are degrees of wickedness. Obviously, to steal a nickel out of mother's purse is not the same as robbing a bank, but both are cut from the same cloth. For a child in a temper tantrum to hit his playmate on the head is not the same as a man having a grudge against an enemy and murdering him, but the spirit is the same. The high schooler who tells his parents he is going to the library to study, but who sneaks in a date with his girlfriend instead is not the same as the man who tells his wife he has an appointment and slips away to see another woman. But they are closely related.

Doing Something about Sin

Just as a slight cold is a warning that all is not well in the body, so unrighteousness, however slight, is a warning that all is not well with a person's morality. "Where envy and self-seeking exist," God says, "confusion and every evil thing will be there" (James 3:16). This is why such reactions within a man should be noted and taken care of. These reactions are *within* him, even though they were stimulated by some circumstance. They can lead to great evil.

We tend to ignore or excuse the inner life. God spoke through the Prophet Ezekiel, saying: "They come to you [Ezekiel] as people do, they sit before you as My people, and they hear your words, but they do not do them; for with their mouth they show much love, but their hearts pursue their own gain" (Ezek. 33:31).

If your anxiety is due to your violation of a biblical principle, then this is good news. It is good news because you can do something about such a violation. You can confess your sin, acknowledge it before the Lord, look at it the same way He looks at it—with hatred and disdain. David admitted his sin before God and asked for cleansing from it: "Wash me thoroughly from my iniquity, and cleanse me from my sin. For I acknowledge my transgressions. . . . Create in me a clean heart, O God. . . . Restore to me the joy of Your salvation" (Ps. 51:2-3a, 10a, 12a).

You cannot erase the past. You cannot decide what your marriage partner will do. You cannot control the conduct of your associates or the turn of world events. But *you can* do something about *your* sin, which cuts you off from personal inner peace.

· This is indeed good news. It is not someone else's wrongs toward you that cause your anxieties and tensions. It is your own sin. And you can do something about it by coming just as you are to God for His forgiveness and cleansing.

The choice is yours.

10
Help for a Hard Journey

Once you have accepted responsibility for your life, you will be tempted to backtrack, to lay the blame for your ups and downs, your troubles and defeats at someone else's door. But don't become discouraged here—or misled. Temptation is something you hold in common with all people. And it too is something you must meet with whatever resources you have and be responsible for your response to it.

What is temptation? Smiley Blanton, noted psychiatrist, offers a good definition:

> Every day of your life, no matter how sheltered you are, you face some choice in which the wrong action is so seductive, so plausible, so pleasurable that it takes a conscious effort of will to reject it. Temptation is universal, as old as the Garden of Eden. Much of your happiness or unhappiness depends on your ability to handle it—instead of letting it handle you ("How to Handle Temptation," *The Reader's Digest,* May 1961, p. 188).

You drive down a highway in a powerful car. The speed signs limit you to 55 miles an hour. But the way is clear; no one is around; you know the car really purrs at 75. The temptation is to step on the gas.

As a Christian, you are committed to give of your income to the Lord, but the furniture is shabby and the sales are on. You are tempted to rationalize withholding your tithe "just this one time."

You have promised to spend the evening with your family. A fellow worker, however, has two tickets to the deciding ball game of a crucial series. He wants you to go with him. You are tempted to go.

Subtle Situations

Temptation does not always appear as a terrible, undesirable evil thing that you won't want to do. You may have little or no problem with something that you aren't interested in doing. But you may be greatly tempted by something you want to do but know you shouldn't. (Or it could be the reverse—something that you should do but don't want to.)

At the moment of temptation, the thing may seem so right. An impulsive purchase that wrecked the household budget seemed so right at the time. To teach a man a lesson who deserved a knuckle-rapping seemed so right in the passion of emotion. So right—except your heart that tells you "it's right" can be so deceitful.

Mrs. Craig, expecting guests, was cleaning the house when the telephone rang. Some friends were meeting downtown for lunch. They wanted to know if she could join them.

"I'd love to meet you, but you know my husband. He's fussy about the way the house looks for company."

"It's just a quick lunch."

"Well, I don't know."

It was a difficult decision. She certainly wanted to join her friends. But should she suit herself or please her husband? She faced temptation.

Mrs. Van Waggoner and her neighbor were golfing. They were about to tee off for the third hole when two men approached the women and asked if they could play through. Mrs. Van Waggoner and her partner readily agreed. But before the men went on, one suggested that the women join them in their game. The women looked at each other. Mrs. Van Waggoner had never faced this situation before. She was quite uneasy about the suggestion, but her neighbor said OK before she could think much about it.

The men proved to be cheerful company—and most attentive. Mrs. Van Waggoner's partner teed up her ball for her, pulled her cart, and helped her improve her iron shots. Perhaps he was a bit too friendly, yet she enjoyed the attention.

After the game the foursome drank iced tea in the clubhouse. As they were about to leave, Mrs. Van Waggoner's partner suggested they have lunch together at a nice little restaurant he knew of. She was tempted—the morning had been so pleasant. To refuse took a definite act of her will, but she did it.

At home she was upset that she had responded so warmly to this strange man. The morning had been filled with temptation, and she wondered what to tell her husband. She found out—as you probably have—that temptation can pop up in the most unexpected places and in the most unusual ways. It can make you aware of desires that take you by surprise.

The Bible says: "Let no man say when he is tempted, 'I am tempted by God'; for God cannot be tempted by evil, nor does He Himself tempt anyone. But each one is tempted when he is drawn away by his own desires and enticed. Then, when desire has conceived, it gives birth to sin; and sin, when it is full grown, brings forth death" (James 1:13-16).

The temptations that bother most people are not those that

would clearly lead into sin. Not many people struggle hard with the temptation to steal. But the semivisible testings are something else. It was not perfectly clear that it was wrong for Mrs. Craig to drop her housecleaning to join her friends downtown. Each person has his own personal, private standards that he has chosen to live by; to fall short is to cause himself personal anxiety. If Mrs. Craig has set for herself a goal of getting the house cleaned and then drops the project, it is likely she will not enjoy the luncheon or get the job done either. The Apostle Paul said: "Happy is he who does not condemn himself in what he approves" (Rom. 14:22).

Everyone faces tempting circumstances constantly. While I was writing this book, I was tempted to lay down my pen and attend a professional golf tournament that was playing in town. To take a break might have been all right, but I had committed myself to a deadline for finishing the manuscript. I resisted the temptation every day but one.

It was an exciting tournament. My enjoyment of it, however, was dampened by the fact that I had left an unfinished task behind. I constantly condemned myself for the thing I had allowed.

Preparing for the Test

In advance of a temptation you must make up your mind not to yield to it. Nevertheless, when temptation comes, you must reaffirm your previously made decision, and this will require a definite act of the will.

Character is forged from encounters with life that tempt you to do wrong. The erring attraction is always present. Paul reminded the Corinthians: "Let him who thinks he stands take heed lest he fall" (1 Cor. 10:12).

It is good for people to compare notes with one another. You may feel that no one faces the same temptation you do. The counselor sees this constantly. The counselee struggles to tell of his temptations. At times, he relates, he overcomes them; at times, he fails. In telling his story he feels that he is revealing something that no one else has ever experienced.

Mr. E., a deacon and sincere Christian, cannot keep his eyes off a woman who recently joined the church.

Mrs. G. is seized with a sudden impulse to slip that nice little knickknack into her purse.

Mrs. H. would like to scratch out her neighbor's eyes because the neighbor won't keep her children out of Mrs. H.'s yard.

The person who thinks he is the only one to face a particular kind of temptation is inclined to justify yielding to it.

"You'd make allowances for my mean disposition if you knew what *I* have to put up with at home," a woman will say, as if there were no other cantankerous husband in the world but her own. And so the story of temptation goes, characterized by these words of Paul: "No temptation has overtaken you except such as is common to man; but God is faithful, who will not allow you to be tempted beyond what you are able, but with the temptation will also make the way to escape, that you may be able to bear it" (1 Cor. 10:13).

Taking the way to escape is your choice, and God is always ready to help you make that choice. But you must remember that your decision on whether or not to yield comes in the face of a wrong action that is so seductive, so plausible, so pleasurable that it takes a conscious act of the will to reject it. The desire to do what you want to do, even though it is wrong, is very strong.

Jesus gave us a strange-sounding formula: "If anyone desires to come after Me, let him deny himself, and take up his cross, and follow Me. For whoever desires to save his life will lose it, and whoever loses his life for My sake will find it" (Matt. 16:24-25). All men are tempted to please only themselves, but the pathway to inner peace is to lose yourself in God's way, to follow Him and do His will at all costs. Inner peace comes to those who seek first the kingdom of God and His righteousness (Matt. 6:33), to those who "pursue righteousness [and] godliness" (1 Tim. 6:11). To enjoy God's peace, you must "pursue the things which make for peace" (Rom. 14:19).

When Temptation Pursues You

Temptations will pursue you even when you seek to determine in what, or in whom, you will put your faith. If you choose the Bible as your guide, there will be those who will try to divert you from it. But God has His "persuaders" too. If you reject the Bible, there will be those who will challenge your decision and seek to "tempt" you to return to God's Word and the things of the Lord. For example, many churches conduct weekly calling programs persuading people to attend Sunday School in order to study the Bible.

In my early 20s I went through a period of rejecting the church, the Bible, and anyone who held to them. It was easy to find people who encouraged me in my rejection. I read educators and psychologists who made it quite clear that man was capable of taking care of himself without crutches such as church and the Bible. Scientific research, they said, would save us.

But others who knew me and who had been helped by the church, the Lord, and a study of His Word were not content to let me rest in this decision. They called on me frequently and exerted great effort to get me to reconsider.

After some years I returned to church and renewed my faith in God and the Bible. During college and graduate school I purposed in my heart, by faith, to use the Bible as my standard for conduct and for evaluating what I heard or read. The Bible was never on trial with me, but the book I was reading or the professor's lecture was. Just as my friends in the church were not content to let my rejection go unchallenged, so my fellow students and professors did not let my decision to accept the Bible as my guide go unchallenged.

"How can you possibly explain putting your faith in the Bible and at the same time be a student of psychology?" they would ask. They tempted me greatly. I wanted my friends and professors to respect and like me. But to have their full respect meant to put my faith where theirs was—in the idea that man is in a process of evolution, in the belief that with our own hands we can build a world of peace.

They never let me forget that every man has a right to choose how he will spend his life and that it is not right for one to impose his standards on another. But as I understood it, the kind of life a man will live is not a matter of his own opinion. For everyone will be judged someday, and the standard for judgment is the Bible. Holding to such a view, I stood alone. How great was the temptation to be like the people around me!

There are writers and speakers, some of them ministers and seminary professors, who are not convinced that the Bible is entirely the Word of God. To consider what they say is to court temptation to give up your reliance on the Bible. Something you read, or hear on the radio or in a speech or in a conversation, or see on television, can tempt you to deviate from what you believe. This will be true whatever course you follow. Having chosen a way for yourself, you will be tempted incessantly to turn from it. And tempting you will be people you admire.

Recently a college student came with a question that troubled him. "Some of the finest people I know are not Christians. They openly spurn the Bible. Yet they seem to be happy and get along well with other people. Some of the leading people in our church are much harder to get along with and do not appear to be as happy as those who are not Christians. If God's way is the only way to peace, then why are these non-Christians peaceful and these Christians not?"

That's a good question. It brings out the point made in the previous chapter, that one's conduct *does* have an impact on others. This young man's faith was being shaken by the conduct of professing Christians. According to his observations, it did not seem to matter if he did not place his faith in Christ and God's Word.

His observations were correct, but you can become confused by observing others. The Bible says: "Do not look at his appearance or at the height of his stature, because I have refused him. For the Lord does not see as man sees; for man looks at the outward appearance, but the Lord looks at the heart" (1 Sam. 16:7).

As a counselor, I see many people who are woefully unhappy individuals but who never give any outward indication of it. A man's outward behavior does not always give a measure of what is going on inside him. God "makes His sun rise on the evil and on the good, and sends rain on the just and on the unjust" (Matt. 5:45). We should be careful about making judgments based on the success or lack of success of others. Paul said: "Let us not judge one another anymore, but rather resolve this, not to put a stumbling block or a cause to fall in our brother's way" (Rom. 14:13).

Whom Will You Trust?

Where will you place your faith? In the conduct of a man? In the words or writings of some individual? Or in God and His Word? You must make this choice alone and then face the ceaseless temptations to change your choice.

Remember the definition offered earlier: You face a choice in which the wrong action is so seductive, so plausible, so pleasurable that it takes a conscious act of will to reject it. In the college student's case, when questions arose about the conduct of Christians and their adjustment to life, it seemed reasonable to turn away from the Bible and to take the viewpoint followed by those who appeared happier. This young man had to make his choice.

Now it is our privilege to "tempt" you with our viewpoint. It is that we have found, and have helped others find, that the Bible is your sure guide to peace.

We have discovered that the man who violates biblical principles will be unhappy, whether he appears to be or not, just as the man who disobeys the rules of health will be sick, whether he looks it or not. We say this by faith. But we say it by experience too. The unhappy, tense, anxious, miserable person who comes to a counselor for help is usually knowingly or unknowingly violating some biblical principle.

How do you approach the God who can give you inner peace? "But without faith it is impossible to please Him, for he who comes to God must believe that He is, and that He is a rewarder of those who diligently seek Him" (Heb. 11:6). Also, "Faith is the substance of things hoped for, the evidence of things not seen" (Heb. 11:1).

You must approach God by faith. You must trust Him fully, with your mind set on Him and His ways. "You [God] will keep him in perfect peace, whose mind is stayed on You, because he trusts in You. Trust in the Lord forever, for in Jehovah, the Lord, is everlasting strength" (Isa. 26:3-4).

As you trust God, He will give you assurance that you are on the right path. But trials, troubles, conflicts, other viewpoints, unexpected failures on your part and on the part of people you admire, will challenge your evidence and throw you back on faith alone. A combination of faith and temptation will make your choice of the Bible as your guide a difficult one to maintain.

The Challenge and the Reward

Let me "tempt" you to make a one-year test of studying and applying to your life what you find in the Bible. To study, to ponder, to test what the Bible says takes time. After all, a student who chooses a psychology career spends four years just getting his bachelor's degree. At that point, he is only a beginner in the field. It also takes time to test the guidance the Bible offers to those who trust God, its author.

"Do not be conformed to this world, but be transformed by the renewing of your mind, that you may prove what is that good and acceptable and perfect will of God" (Rom. 12:2). This verse implies knowledge of God's Word and love for and obedience to that knowledge. We do not propose a simple, easy approach to inner peace. It is a struggle, with a starting point based on simple faith, with many temptations along the way to draw you aside, on a pathway that today is rejected by many serious, dedicated, sincere people.

The reward is still there for those who take God's way, in spite of the difficulties. And there is help along the route. Prayer is the gateway to getting this help from God.

> Let us therefore come boldly to the throne of grace, that we may obtain mercy and find grace to help in time of need (Heb. 4:16).
>
> Entertain no worry, but under all circumstances let your petitions be made known before God by prayer and pleading along with thanksgiving. So will the peace of God, that surpasses all understanding, keep guard over your hearts and your thoughts in Christ Jesus (Phil. 4:6-7, MLB).

Jesus said, "If you shall ask anything in My name, I will do it" (John 14:14). And He followed this with these words: "If you love Me, keep My commandments" (John 14:15).

If you want your prayers for help answered, become familiar with the commands of God in the Bible. Verbalize your longings before God, then wait to see what He will do. If you have asked according to His will (that is, if you have prayed with the desire that *His* will may be done), you will have what you asked for. It is yours if it fits into God's plan. And remember that His ways are not necessarily your ways (Isa. 55:8-9). But also, His ways are not grievous or burdensome (1 John 5:3).

Your challenge is to accept the Bible as your guide and to obey God's commands fully. If you do, you will find that the Bible is a mirror in which you see yourself as you really are. And when you see yourself, what you do is *still* up to you. You can correct what ought to be corrected. But you will be tempted to look away and forget what you saw (James 1:23-25). And in looking away you will soon become absorbed in counterattractions that will not let you return for a second look.

But if by faith you go God's way, you will find inner peace along the way as well as at the end of the road. "He who wants to enjoy life and see happy days must keep his tongue from speaking evil and his lips from uttering deceit. He must turn away from wrong and do right; he must search for peace and keep after it. For the Lord's eyes are on the righteous and His ears are attentive to their prayer, but the Lord's face is set against those who practice evil" (1 Peter 3:10-12, MLB).

11
One More Time

Educators tell us that repetition aids learning. In your quest to find inner peace and a quiet heart, it is well to be reminded that the peace we refer to in this book comes only from God and is freely given to all who qualify to call God their "Father."

I also want to be sure you understand the Gospel, which is the gateway or access to God. Many, many people have appealed to God for peace but there is no response. The best explanation for this silence is explained in the Bible: "Behold, the Lord's hand is not shortened, that it cannot save; nor His ear heavy, that it cannot hear. But your iniquities have separated you from your God; and your sins have hidden His face from you" (Isa. 59:1-2). The psalmist said: "If I regard iniquity in my heart, the Lord will not hear" (Ps. 66:18).

A Call to Salvation
It is your sins that come between you and God. This is where the Gospel comes in. The Apostle Paul wrote to the Corinthians: "I delivered to you first of all that which I also received:

that Christ died for our sins according to the Scriptures, and that He was buried, and that He rose again the third day according to the Scriptures" (1 Cor. 15:3-4). To the Ephesians, Paul exclaimed: "For through Him [Jesus Christ] we both have access by one Spirit to the Father" (Eph. 2:18).

Jesus explained to His disciples: "I am the way, the truth, and the life. No one comes to the Father except through Me" (John 14:6). Jesus also said, "Behold, I stand at the door and knock. If anyone hears My voice and opens the door, I will come in to him and dine with him, and he with Me" (Rev. 3:20).

Finally, Peter said it clearly to a Jerusalem crowd gathered on the Day of Pentecost: "Repent therefore and be converted, that your sins may be blotted out, so that times of refreshing may come from the presence of the Lord" (Acts 3:19).

If you sense a stirring in your heart and have never done so, open the door of your heart, and He will come in, blot out your sins, and give you access to the Father. Then, and only then, will you be able to ask for God's supernatural peace.

A Call to Christians

You may be a Christian. That is, you have invited Jesus to come into your life as your Saviour. He has forgiven your sins and you have experienced His peace. Now, however, He seems very distant. Perhaps a root of bitterness troubles you. Perhaps you are nursing hatred, resentment, malice, or anger toward someone who has misused you. There is something between you and God, and only biblical advice can clear away the fog that makes Him seem far away: "Let the wicked forsake his way, and the unrighteous man his thoughts; let him return to the Lord, and He will have mercy on him; and to our God, for He will abundantly pardon" (Isa. 55:7).

In closing, consider two beautiful promises God makes to His people. They can be yours if you obey Him:

I will give you a new heart and put a new spirit within you; I will take the heart of stone out of your flesh and give you a heart of flesh. I will put My Spirit within you and cause you to walk in My statutes, and you will keep My judgments and do them (Ezek. 36:26-27).

For I know the thoughts that I think toward you, says the Lord, thoughts of peace and not of evil, to give you a future and a hope. Then you will call upon Me and go and pray to Me, and I will listen to you. And you will seek Me and find Me when you search for Me with all your heart (Jer. 29:11-13).

Be assured that God will do His part when you obey Him. And your struggle for inner peace will be won.